Earthy, with a Hint of Cucumber will bring out your inner water geek as surely as a travelogue by Bill Bryson will draw you to the airline ticket counter. This book is an excellent introduction to the love of water for virtually any age group.

~ **Steve Via**
American Water Works Association

The perfect companion to a refreshing glass of drinking water is not ice, but this fascinating expedition into the chemistry, ecology, tastes, odors, sights, and sounds of water. Our appreciation and knowledge of the voyage of water from river to house and mouth are much enhanced by this enjoyable book.

~ **Andrea Dietrich, PhD**
Professor of Civil and Environmental Engineering
Virginia Tech

Earthy, with a Hint of Cucumber tells the story of the author's path to a career in water. His passion and dedication for his profession, and his sense of being part of something larger and more important than a job come across very clearly on these pages. At a time when young scientists and engineers have an unprecedented number of career options, the importance of sharing stories like this one, and of using these stories to attract the next generation of water professionals, has never been greater. This book is both a very enjoyable read and an example for those of us in the water community to follow.

~ **Chris Rayburn**
Director of Research and Subscriber Services
Water Research Foundation

Earthy, with a Hint of Cucumber encourages me, as a young professional engineer, to take an intriguing journey; to walk along, to sense, to wonder, and to imagine further. As with a clue, a detective solves a mystery. So with a hint of odor, a scientist traces a problem to its very source. This book is about more than the smell and taste of water; it's about the sense and sensibility of a career.

~ **Lijie Li, PhD, PE**
Project Engineer
KCI Technologies, Inc.

Earthy, with a Hint of Cucumber is the fascinating account of the unexpected career path of one of the pioneers in taste and odor research in drinking water. What began as a research project—to look at what was causing bad tastes in Philadelphia's tap water—resulted in an amazing life-long career as a water-quality scientist. The book reads like a detective thriller—and includes both historical references and personal experiences—describing in understandable language the science involved in determining the causes of tastes and odors in drinking water. For newly minted college grads in engineering and science, wondering what interesting and fulfilling professions might be out there, this book gives readers a glimpse of where a career path in the drinking water field can lead.

~ **Jennifer L. Clancy, PhD, MS Law**
Chief Scientist
Corona Environmental Consulting, LLC

In *Earthy, with a Hint of Cucumber*, Gary Burlingame adroitly portrays how he became a taste and smell water connoisseur and devout "water geek." This book presents technical scientific concepts in relatable, easily understood language. It should be a must-read for engineers contemplating or perusing water-related engineering.

~ **Michael Ryan, PhD**
Assistant Teaching Professor of Civil, Architectural,
and Environmental Engineering
Drexel University

EARTHY,
WITH A HINT OF
CUCUMBER

Gary A. Burlingame

EARTHY, WITH A HINT OF CUCUMBER
Copyright © 2015 by Gary A. Burlingame

Published by:

Peak Publishing
9375 Blue Mountain Drive • Golden, CO 80403
peakpublishinginfo@gmail.com

Author: Gary A. Burlingame
Designer: Judy Johnson

Printed in the United States of America

Library of Congress Cataloging-in-Publication Data
Burlingame, Gary A.

ISBN **978-1-519244-22-2**
1. Biography & Autobiography / Personal Memoirs;
2. Biography & Autobiography / Science & Technology;
3. Biography & Autobiography / Environmentalists & Naturalists

Most Peak Publishing resources are available worldwide through bookstores and
online outlets, depending on their format. Primary distribution for this book and
its Kindle-formatted eBook is through *www.Amazon.com*. This book also can be
obtained directly from the publisher in printed and eBook formats, including
PDF, ePub, and Kindle. Contact *peakpublishinginfo@gmail.com* for information on how to order single or multiple copies, with free shipping,
or eBook versions not available elsewhere. Redistribution of printed
or eBook formatted copies violates international copyright
law, and is strictly forbidden, although purchasers of
eBooks may print one copy per title for
their own personal use.

ACKNOWLEDGEMENTS

A valuable, rewarding career journey involves friends, co-workers, and teachers who coach us and encourage us, and share in our experiences. I have been fortunate to be surrounded by many such people. Co-workers at the Philadelphia Water Department contributed greatly to the richness of my journey. Others, from around the world, have also been important to me. The following, listed in alphabetical order, stand out: Auguste Bruchet, Roy Desrochers, Andrea Dietrich, Richard Doty, Thomas Gittelman, Robert Hoehn, Djanette Khiari, Harvey Minnigh, Wesley Pipes, Graciela Ramirez-Toro, Mel Suffet, Mark Waer, and Sue Watson. The Water Research Foundation supported much of our research. The American Water Works Association brought like-minded people together. And the International Water Association provided a global connection.

CONTENTS

FOREWORD

Throughout my many years as a water professional, I have been extremely fortunate to have had the opportunity to travel the world and meet so many of the outstanding people involved in this incredible and vital industry. Gary's book, through the finest tradition of storytelling, brings to life the essence of those dedicated individuals in the water field that I have had the privilege to get to know in my travels.

Winston Churchill once said: "We make a living by what we get, but we make a life by what we give." It is clear by Gary's personal account of his professional journey, that he has been living a full and rewarding life. And, throughout this account of his fulfilling journey, Gary has modeled a noble and key characteristic of most of those in the water industry—"service above self-interest." Gary has certainly given of himself for the benefit of the environment and public safety in his life's work, and is again giving back to our industry by masterfully sharing his story in a way that will surely entertain, and, more importantly, inspire others to consider a career in this exciting industry.

I'm sure that many of us, either before or at the start of our careers, may remember how a specific opportunity presented to us sparked a strong interest or even ignited a passion in us to pursue a career in the water industry. That's why you should read this book—it just may present that type of memorable opportunity for you.

In describing his journey in the industry, Gary writes: "I was assigned to discover what it was about Philadelphia's tap water that caused. . . ." Then, like in a classic detective novel, he takes us on an enlightening ride through the world of water, not only discussing what we already know about the importance of water, but introducing elements that we may not have considered before, such as his description about noticing the elusive scent of "an unusual top note" when it appeared in the water of one of the city's drinking water treatment plants.

Along the way, Gary also shares valuable nuggets of information and offers to the reader the significant knowledge that he gained though his vast experience and the contributions he has made within the industry, both at his utility and through industry research organizations. When you finish reading this book, you will indeed want to recommend it to those both within and outside of our industry so that they, too, can gain a better understanding of this remarkable industry. You may also arrive at the same conclusion I did, recognizing how fortunate we are to have committed professionals like Gary keeping a watchful eye on our precious drinking water resources.

I believe we are at a unique point in time in the history of our profession, where we now have a majority of "seasoned practitioners" in the twilight of their careers. Of course, as they exit the industry, there will be vast amounts of experience and knowledge that will be leaving with them as well. It's critical that we have enough water professionals ready to take the place of those "seasoned practitioners" within our industry. Certainly, Gary has set the example to follow for all of us who are as passionate about this industry as he is. We need to share our stories, to transfer knowledge that only a "seasoned" water professional can, as well as motivate and inspire others to take on long-term careers in the water field.

As Gary demonstrates in the book, storytelling is a very powerful learning tool that has the added power to transform and ignite passion for a noble profession such as ours. Telling these stories promotes our identity as an industry and will pass on our culture to subsequent generations. And, it represents our collective memory of those who have contributed so much to make our industry what it is today. Clearly, stories can provide understanding of why things are the way they are; they link the past to the present; and they can provide the foundation for dedicated young professionals to take on this responsibility for the future.

Once upon a time, there was a passionate, dedicated environmental scientist named Gary who lived and worked in a major eastern city and had a life's journey like no other, and fortunately, he was willing to share his story. . . .

~ **Andrew W. Richardson**
Chairman and CEO
Greeley and Hansen
AWWA President – 2005

Preface

WHILE WATER PROFESSIONALS PUBLISH AND PRESENT THEIR TECH-nical knowledge in journals and at conferences, they share their personal stories during coffee breaks and around the dinner table. Their stories reveal the heart and soul of our profession. In *Earthy, with a Hint of Cucumber*, I share my story.

What started out as a year or two of laboratory experiments became a lifelong journey that took me back in time and around the world. I found myself investing in something more than a career, than a job title, or a paycheck. I became part of something bigger, more lasting, and more valuable.

So where are you? What journey are you on? Are you investing in something bigger and more lasting, more valuable than you could ever imagine? Maybe someday we'll hear your story. I hope so!

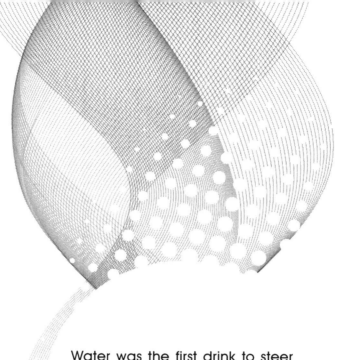

Water was the first drink to steer the course of human history; now, after ten thousand years, it seems to be back in the driving seat.

~ Tom Standage[1]

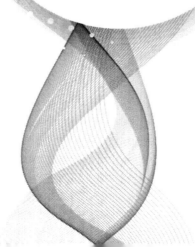

Chapter 1

Going with the Flow

WATER FLOWED THROUGHOUT MY EVERYDAY LIFE BUT I JUST TOOK it for granted. We swam at the public pool on boy's day. We took baths once or twice a week. At the hatcheries we put worms on our hooks to catch catfish. In the driveway we loaded water pistols for shootouts. All of this water around me but I don't remember drinking much of it. I guzzled soda pop. I was addicted to the carbonation's sting in my throat. I chugged it the way Canadians drink beer: *It goes down so quickly it never touches the taste buds.*

Growing up, especially as a boy, we spit. There was an art to

> Growing up, especially as a boy, we spit. There was an art to it, like whistling. Some boys had a natural ability. But we didn't know that our spit was best kept in our mouths.

it, like whistling. Some boys had a natural ability. But we didn't know that our spit was best kept in our mouths. It is mostly water, a type of mineral water. No one told us that it is important for our health.[2] It protects our teeth, lubricates and moves food to our sensory receptors, bathes our taste buds, keeps anaerobic bacteria under control, and provides enzymes to break down the carbs in Philly's famous soft pretzels. When you are thirsty your spit dries up and your mouth tells your brain you need a drink. A dry mouth causes a diminished sense of taste which in turn affects your diet, which in turns affects your health. You can place an object in your mouth to stimulate spit production, or cold water and ice, or something that tastes sour.[3]

It was thirst that made me appreciate water. While hiking the Appalachians or through the Pine Barrens, there was no room for cans of soda in our backpacks. My mom's homemade chocolate chip cookies, yes, but soda was too heavy. My brother and I carried canteens we purchased from the army and navy store. We filled them at mountain springs and cedar swamps. And the water was cool and it tasted refreshing.

It was a time when a postage stamp cost less than a nickel. The first US satellite launched into outer space. Alaska became a state. Huckleberry Hound and Yogi Bear cartoons entertained us on black and white TV. No one owned a personal computer or a cell phone. And water was very cheap. My dad let me water the lawn for an hour, holding my thumb over the nozzle to squirt the bees and drench the marigold flowers. During the muggy days of summer, all across the city, fire hydrants dropped their iron caps to gush water into the streets because it was safe to play in the streets.

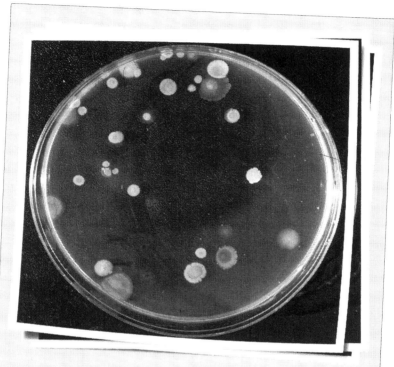

My scientific research began with studying the microbiological life in water using techniques that encourages it to grow on agar until it can be seen. Today, using molecular methods that test for genetic material, we are redefining what lives in the water we drink.

As an undergraduate student, I volunteered in the university's research lab. Grad students were studying the microscopic life of drinking water. It was interesting to me and it seemed important. I was taught to wash my hands with water to remove germs and dirt. I had never thought about bacteria in water. So I guess I assumed that the water was always free of them. In the lab, with my growing curiosity, I wanted to create a pictorial atlas of the bacteria found in tap water. So we lured bacteria out of water by placing them on agar with food in it. Here they reproduced and formed colonies, or little bacterial cities of unique architecture—different colors and textures and shapes like human cities. Some bacterial colonies were small and pink, pimple shaped. Others formed white swirls that spread across the agar. Colors ranged from white, yellow, and orange to brown; this diversity of the bacteria changed with the seasons of the year. Water temperature was one driving force for this.

For most of human history, we did not know about the unseen world of microbes. It was the study of the smells of fermentation and decay that provided fertile material for scientists to explore the processes of life and death in which water plays a role. It was obvious that boiling water, then filtering and decanting off the top to leave the sediment behind made the water look and taste better, thereby making it healthier. In this way, the human senses were used to judge water's benefit to health.

Pliny wrote about the value of healthy water and the Greek physician and father of medicine, Hippocrates, believed from his study of body fluids that water was very important to our health.[4] He believed that the human body had four critical humors or fluids that must remain in balance to keep us healthy. Hippocrates tasted water and believed that the taste could tell something about its healthfulness. The "Hippocratic Sleeve," or water and wine filter, is a cloth bag that traps sediment after water is boiled.

When the "Germ Theory" of disease fought its way into our textbooks at the turn of the 20th century, it battled against the belief in miasmas or foul odors and poisonous vapors that were thought to cause death. When it became clear that stinky water may not contain harmful germs but that water free of smell could be teaming with life-threatening microbes, we lost trust in our senses to separate the good from the bad. Scientists replaced the human senses with bacteriological culturing of microorganisms and chemical testing for ammonia, oxygen, sulfur, and other gases.

Today, molecular testing of RNA and DNA has redefined what lives in the air we breathe and the water we drink. What I once grew on agar cultures misled me into thinking I had captured the demographics. Consider trying to describe the people of New York City based solely on who eats hot dogs or tofu for lunch. Water contains a variety of bacteria classified as Alphaproteobacteria, Betaproteobacteria, and Gammaproteobacteria. These include such genera as *Sphingomonas*, *Klebsiella*, *Pseudomonas*, *Mycobacterium*, and *Nitrosomonas*. They prefer different growth conditions and different food. Fortunately, before I got too far, my boss asked me to try fixing another problem with water. I thought, *I'll put in a year or two and then get back to what really matters.* Since bacteria had defined the safety of water, or the water's healthfulness, then I must have been on the right track.

I was assigned to discover what it was about Philadelphia's tap water that caused the people of the City of Brotherly Love to complain. I didn't know there was a problem with the water although I grew up in Philadelphia. My parents were transplants from Michigan, and they never said anything bad about the tap water to me. Nonetheless, the Water Commissioner was tired of hearing complaints

> I was assigned to discover what it was about Philadelphia's tap water that caused the people of the City of Brotherly Love to complain.

and so he decided to take action and do something about it. This challenge required more than an understanding of chemistry and microbiology; it required that I take a trip back in time and learn the art of using the human senses to unravel the mysteries of water flavor.

I pointed to the river and asked my host, "How hard is it to treat that water?" The river was full and flowing fast, running downhill through forested hills from a protected reservoir high up in the mountains. Its color was clay red. It was full of sediment. I could not imagine a water treatment plant having an easy time removing all that sediment. But they explained that being inorganic silt, it was easier to treat than organic sediment from farmlands. The bigger challenge to them was what happens to the water after the treatment is done. As the drinking water travels out into the city, buildings and homes store it in rooftop water tanks. The tanks provide a consistent water supply with adequate water pressure to each building. But in the tanks, sitting on the rooftops in the full sun, the water sits and incubates, suspended matter collects, and the water goes bad. What we see and what appears obvious is not always what we need to focus our attention on. Sometimes the real challenges are hidden from view.

Your body is about 80 percent water and most of it is hidden from view. Six weeks you can survive without food, but only one week without water. Water lubricates joints, supports immune systems, helps in food digestion, maintains body temperature, transports nutrients and oxygen, flushes out waste, and bathes the brain. Water enters the body directly by water consumption as well as through beverages and food. It escapes the body through waste and urine, breathing and sweating.

I was a physically active boy. We did not have video games, cable TV, the Internet, or computers to keep us indoors. We played baseball, basketball, wire ball, stick ball, and half ball during the summer. And we sweated a lot. But it never bothered us. Today—that's a different story. Sweat is annoying. It stings my eyes. It gets on my glasses. And I don't have to do much to bring it on. Nonetheless, it is vitally important.

Our human bodies must maintain a balance in water and temperature. Thus, athletes avoid heat stroke by sweating. Sweating rids the body of water and salt, and the water carries off heat. Elderly people can die from failing to cool their bodies during the summer because they don't sweat like they did when they were younger. Our body's warning signs tell us when we need water. The signs of dehydration include dry lips, dry skin, muscle cramps, headaches, nausea, vomiting, and digestion problems. And when we have diarrhea or are vomiting, we must remember to replace the water we've lost.

While we can die from maintaining too little water, we can also die from drinking too much water. And that's not by drowning. Taking in too much water over a short period of time, combined with our body's inability to get rid of the excess, causes a loss in the salt content of body tissue. The salts of sodium and potassium help maintain blood pressure and the functioning of muscles and nerves in our heart and brain. As the salt content inside our body's cells exceed what's in the blood, the cells swell by taking on excess water to offset osmotic pressure. The brain swells against the skull and brain stem. This brings about confusion, loss of consciousness, coma, and even death. This is called water intoxication or hyponatremia.

However, water, just plain safe water, is the best beverage to consume and we should

> However, water, just plain safe water, is the best beverage to consume and we should drink plenty of water every day.

drink plenty of water every day.[5] Some experts go so far as to claim that we are chronically dehydrated, experiencing daytime fatigue, joint pain, and digestion difficulties, and an increased risk of cancer. In 1945, the US Food and Nutrition Board developed a rule-of-thumb for the consumption of water known as the 8x8 rule: an adult should drink eight, 8-ounce glasses or 1.89 liters of water a day.[6,7] The US Department of Health and Human Services, in 1989, found that on average, including what we eat such as fruits and vegetables which consist of up to 80 percent water, we take in 2.1 liters of water every day of which 1.2 liters is tap water.[8] In 2005, the National Academy of Sciences reported[9] that a well-hydrated woman takes in 2.7 liters of total water every day, or about 11 glasses of water. A well-hydrated man takes in 3.7 liters, or about 15½ glasses of water. Around 80 percent of this water comes from beverages, the rest comes from food. Thus it seems that we are consuming adequate amounts of water. And we should drink continually throughout the day without waiting for our thirst to trigger it.

We constantly make choices on how we stay hydrated. Various sources of water have played important roles in the history of the world.[10] On coming to the pristine forests of America, the colonists distrusted the natural streams. So they brought beer and rum and other drink for hydration. Through the 1600s, 1700s, and 1800s these drinks provided for healthy voyages across the Atlantic and back, as well as for successful naval battles. Because beer, wine, coffee, and tea require the boiling of water or addition of alcohol at some point in their production, these beverages saved many lives from waterborne diseases throughout human history.

Today we have empires built on bottled water, from mineral and sparkling waters to spring and purified tap waters; waters that come from aquifers, springs, public supplies, rain, glaciers, and even icebergs. Such bottled water is marketed around the world for our convenience, taste, and perceptions of healthfulness. Their flavors vary according to carbonation and total dissolved solids which affect the mouth feel of the water.[11] Imagine describing your drinking water as *crisp, smooth, rejuvenating, bold,* or *explosive.* This is how you might describe bottled mineral water.

However, the pure water in a bottle may not always be as beneficial to drink on a regular basis. Urban, low income minorities may choose it over tap water for drinking and for infant formula preparation, even in developed countries that have safe tap water. Some parents give purified bottled water to their children in infancy.[12] Yet the lack of key minerals in some waters can be bad for children's health. Nonetheless, people in developing countries may prefer bottled water, rejecting the cheaper public water supply.

Since Evian started the craze in 1829, bottled water sales have grown such that an average person might use 30 liters in a year despite it costing 240 to 10,000 times more than tap water.[13] Mexico and Italy are big consumers of bottled water. A gallon of tap water might cost less than one penny compared to bottled water for $1.00 or much more.[14]

Water is vital for life. It's no surprise that the world's civilizations have rituals, customs, art, law, and economies based on water in one way or another. It is indeed worthy of a lifetime's endeavor to protect and preserve!

Although water is essential for life, many people still don't have access to safe drinking water. I take it for granted. I

> Although water is essential for life, many people still don't have access to safe drinking water. I take it for granted.

wake up in the morning, stumble into the bathroom, and turn on the tap with full expectation that clean water will come out. However, around the world, children are dying from a lack of safe water, or just clean water to wash their faces and hands. Water is so important to life that the United Nation's Millennium Development Goals[15] included halving the number of people worldwide who don't have access to safe drinking water and basic sanitation. In 2010, the UN General Assembly and Human Rights Council set a resolution declaring safe drinking water and sanitation a human right, essential to the full enjoyment of life and all human rights. The World Health Organization reported, in 2014, that 2.5 billion people lack the ability to regularly wash with soap and water; that 1.8 billion rely on water that is contaminated with fecal waste. The decade of 2005 to 2015 was declared "The Decade of Water for Life." That's how important water is!

But who has the right to control the water cycle; the springs and the water deep in the ground, the free flowing streams, and the natural lakes? The increasing demand for this limited resource is growing every day such that people are trading water rights, or changing the rights that have been around since America was settled. In some places, too much water is being taken out of the ground. What about wastewater? We put treated wastewater back into the water cycle from which we draw water for drinking. This is called indirect, unintentional reuse. Or we pump wastewater back into the ground and let it be treated naturally as it percolates through soil and sand before coming out in wells. Or we use modern technology to treat wastewater for direct potable reuse, for drinking! Since we can desalinate water, how will that change the way we manage the ocean?

The responsibility for the nation's water has traditionally been divided among different agencies. Wastewater is managed by a different office than drinking water. Atmospheric water is managed by different people than those who manage groundwater or water for agriculture, than those who manage water for recreation or the oceans. And water in home plumbing differently than water in flood control reservoirs. We cannot be good stewards of the water cycle by managing it from our silos of narrow vision. Add to this the fear of climate change. Only a 4°C rise in global air temperature could be catastrophic, especially if it happens over a short period of time, say a hundred years. We would not have enough time to adjust—to relocate our cities away from the rising water levels. Some places on earth will be inundated with water while others will be drying up from a lack of water. Slowly, by necessity, the responsibility for water is changing. The business model, the design, the regulation, the very value of water is changing. We call this *One Water* or *Total Water Management.*

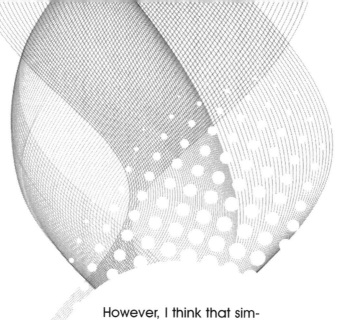

However, I think that simple awareness of how amazing, wonderful, and incredible our sense of smell is, and how much pleasure, dimensionality, intensity, and meaning it can bring to our lives, is the most essential olfactory knowledge that we need to enrich our lives now and in the future.

~ Rachel Herz[1]

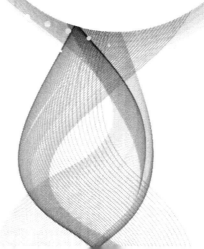

Chapter 2

Learning to Smell

Growing up, I didn't pay much attention to my senses but I know today that I would not have enjoyed my youth without them. Hearing, feeling, seeing, smelling, and tasting were all part of growing up. The catch of the football, the finger-tip toss of the basketball, and the gentle bite of a perch on the fishing line. The smell of campfire, of baking bread, and of my leather baseball glove. The mouth-feel of crispy potato chips or the burn on the tongue from fresh-from-the-oven brownies. The flavor of a handful of buttered popcorn dotted with pieces of sweet chocolate.

I now know that my senses are important to me. Back then I didn't give it any thought. There are possible reasons why I might not have paid attention to the way things smelled and tasted. Ageusia is the inability to taste. Anosmia is the inability to smell. But I didn't have these conditions; I just wasn't paying attention to my senses.

My wife and I rented a condo in New Orleans, in the French Quarter. We had to carry our luggage up three flights of stairs to get to it. There was no elevator. The stairs were old and wooden.

And they had a particular smell that reminded me of my grandfather's big, old house in Michigan's Upper Peninsula. The smell brought back visual memories from my childhood, such as lying in bed during the early morning hours with the covers up to my neck while the house frightened me with its creaky sounds and echoes. The connection that's established between smell and memories—especially bad memories—is very strong. It can be awakened without us consciously knowing it. Our brain is wired this way.

There was no class in high school that taught me about my sensory systems or how to hone my skills at using them. So when I began to study Philadelphia's tap water I had to learn from scratch. I found out that there is a technique to tasting—listen, look, sip, slurp, swish, chew, and swallow. First, pour the water into a glass and listen to the sound it makes. Swirl it and observe its clarity. Sip so as not to overwhelm your senses. Slurp like you are annoying your mother with bad manners at dinner time. Chew as if to crack it open to free the aroma from inside. Swish it around in your mouth to contact all your nerve endings and taste buds before you swallow. Taste cells coat your tongue and are scattered around your mouth as well as in your stomach and intestines, helping drive your body's need for nutrients and steering digestion. This is what tasting snobs do. Try it. You will develop a deeper appreciation for whatever you chow down on at lunch time. And if you take your time, you will give your taste buds a chance to communicate with your brain.

Our brain connects with our five tastes to benefit our health. Bitter warns us of poison. Sour alerts us to rotting and fermenting fruit. A salty taste encourages us to consume electrolytes that are vital to our body's communication system. Sweet draws us to carbohydrates, which babies are particularly in need of for rapid growth. Umami—the fifth taste—to amino acids, the building blocks of proteins which support the architecture of our bodies. There is a possible sixth taste—the taste of fats or fatty acids—which may be the taste that most affects obesity. But it is also the taste that makes grilled hamburgers so good tasting.

If you were to say, "My water tastes like a swimming pool," what you mean to say is that it *smells* like a pool. When you take water into your mouth, you warm it and swish it around before sending it down your throat. This liberates odors into the cavern of your mouth to sweep up the back flue or retronasal passage to your olfactory smelling center. This retronasal passage is where the annoying post-nasal drip takes place. Thus you smell what you take into your mouth. If you don't believe me, try this. With two fingers, clamp off your nose. This will prevent air in your mouth from rising up your retronasal passageway. Place seasoned croutons or flavored cough drops in your mouth with your nose held closed. What do you sense? Quite bland. Now do this again, but once the food is in your mouth, close your mouth and release your nose, breathing deeply through it. Wow! A burst of flavor! You smell what you eat.

> Though we talk about how things taste, it's just a lazy way of speaking about flavor. Flavor comprises the five tastes along with mouth feel and aroma.

Though we talk about how things taste, it's just a lazy way of speaking about flavor. Flavor comprises the five tastes along with mouth feel and aroma. If you were to complain, "My water tastes funny today," or "I don't like the way my water tastes," what you really mean to say is the water's *flavor* is bad.

Then there is aftertaste—the flavor that stays around after you swallow. Water is supposed to be refreshing—cool and with no aftertaste. Did you ever drink rusty water? It leaves a lingering metallic flavor. I first experienced it in third grade, drinking from the school fountains during outdoor recess. The metallic aftertaste was not a good complement to my chocolate treats. Most foods, however, have an aftertaste because the residual sensation keeps you coming back for more. Imagine what ice cream would be like if as soon as you swallowed it, the flavor disappeared.

Finally, we have the sensation of touch. The texture or feel of what you eat also affects your enjoyment of it. Imagine eating a soggy potato chip or biting into limp celery. Many foods make crispy, crunchy, and crackly sounds when we eat them, and these sounds influence our enjoyment of them. My wife and I had a young woman over for dinner to hear about her years in Africa. We offered her a salad made with fresh, crispy Iceberg lettuce. She was so excited. It had been a long time since she was able to enjoy a good salad. In Africa, where she lived, lettuce and vegetables were soaked in bleach, and it robbed them of their fresh crispiness. This is a common problem around the world with vegetables irrigated with fecal waste-contaminated water. If consumers don't wash or disinfect the vegetables thoroughly, they can get very sick.

While water doesn't or shouldn't have a feeling to it—it is not crunchy or crispy—it can elicit feeling sensations. Water can feel drying, or astringent, or as if it's leaving a coating in your mouth. Mineral waters give you some of these mouth feels. Mineral waters are waters that are high in salts, carbonates, and sulfates. Europeans pay a lot of money to drink mineral water.

The process of smelling is amazingly complex; it holds many mysteries for us even today. Odor molecules must be airborne and inhaled into the nasal cavity to come in contact with the olfactory neurons that produce a signal for the olfactory bulb which communicates with the brain for interpretation, memory development, expression, and reaction. It is a process, as engineers would say, with various links that can go wrong. For example, your nose can perceive phantom smells that don't really exist. This is called *phantosmia*. Some smell problems are due to other issues. Parkinson's Disease interferes with smelling because motor movement is affected, which decreases one's ability to sniff. Blocked nasal passages are a common problem as they prevent the contact of odor molecules with the sensory system.

Smelling, as well as other senses, are at their optimum when we are newly born. Then it's all downhill from there. Just as our ability to distinguish sound decreases as the ear is exposed to noise, and as sight weakens with time, the sense of smell weakens as we grow older. I wish I had better news, but those are the facts. And since the olfactory sensors in our nose lie physically close to our brain, injuries and infections can cause temporary or permanent damage. Imagine having to live without being able to smell anything at all.

Did you ever wonder why the human nose has two holes or nostrils? Maybe it simply looks better that way since the nose lies between two eyes. It could be a body symmetry thing. But we don't smell the same through each nostril; we favor one or rotate the use of nostrils throughout the day. Try this. Lie down on your side and notice how the opposite nostril opens up, compensating for the one that is pressed against the pillow.

Rabbits have about twenty times more receptors for smelling than humans.[2] Have you ever seen a rabbit's nose twitch? The faster the nose twitches, the better the rabbit exposes air to its smell receptors. When excited, its nose may twitch six times faster than when it is calm.

Our noses don't twitch. We sniff. To *sniff* literally means to smell

Water has a shelf life just like any food or beverage. Once it is produced, it should be stored in clean containers, kept out of the sunlight, and maintained at a cool temperature. Objectionable tastes and odors can develop with the regrowth of microorganisms and the corrosion of the packaging materials it is in contact with.

or to inhale through the nose. First sniffs or first impressions are the most reliable. And since everyone's nasal passageway is unique in its physical construction, you inherently learn to sniff in your own optimum way; long drawn out sniffs are not natural. An optimum sniff takes in about 200 cubic centimeters of air at a rate of thirty liters per minute in only about one half of a second.[3] Fortunately, if that sniff is too strong or unpleasant an experience then your brain will tune it down like muting the volume on the TV. All of this happens, constantly, as you move about your world of constant sensory stimulation.

When I come home from work and open the door to my house, I sniff the air that rushes out without even thinking about it. If the air smells as I last smelled it, then I proceed inside without thinking. But if I smell the warning odorant spiked in natural gas, then my brain says, "STOP!" Or if I smell garbage, I wonder: *Who didn't take out the trash?* We are constantly smelling, making decisions, and processing the sensory information that comes in through our nose.

Your brain learns new associations or reinforces existing memories every time you sniff[4] because the place where emotions and memories are processed gets stimulated. Even back to being a newborn baby, smells are hyperlinked to experiences. These hyperlinks initiate rapid automatic responses before your mind has a chance to think about what you are smelling. Thinking only slows down the mental process.

Back when you were a baby, before your parents imparted to you their likes and dislikes, you probably liked the smell of your poop and you may have found rancid cheese to be pleasant.[5] Then your parents taught you, through voice inflection and facial expression, that some smells are bad. And bad smells, or smells linked to bad experiences, got imprinted into your brain quite readily and permanently.

I can't recall what my home smelled like when I was growing up.

> When I visited other boy's homes, they smelled different from mine. Smells of old furniture, of plastic slip covers, or dog. But *my* house didn't smell —at least it didn't smell to me.

When I visited other boy's homes, they smelled different from mine. Smells of old furniture, of plastic slip covers, or dog. But *my* house didn't smell —at least it didn't smell to me. That's called sensory adaptation. It's when your senses stop noticing something, such as when you look around for where you left your sunglasses, and they're on top of your head. You stopped feeling the glasses. You adapted to the feeling.

It is theoretically possible to train your brain to recognize from 10,000 odorous chemicals to more than a trillion sensory stimulations induced by smelling.[5,6] If you are a perfumer or fragrancer, it would be your job to describe what you smell and so you would be highly trained to identify odors down to their chemical names. Yet when someone asks you, "Do you smell that?" and you do, perhaps you try to talk about what you smell but you can't describe it. It smells familiar but you just can't place it. We call that a tip-of-the-nose experience. If I were to give you a list of descriptions of what you might be smelling, so you don't have to reach back into your memory, you would probably put a name to it quite readily. In the second century, Greek physician Galen characterized everything he smelled as either hot, cold, dry, or wet. Now that makes no sense to us today. But to him, these were the four foundations of our sense of smell.[7]

With all of what we know today about how the sense of smell works, we still call it subjective, or that it depends on individual perceptions and preferences. Perhaps that's because we are quite variable. We vary from morning to night, day to day, and as we grow older.[8] We are not laboratory instruments that have a demonstrated level of accuracy and precision every time we use our senses. We are not that easily controlled. The human sensory system forgets its calibration even with extensive, ongoing training. Thus, when we want to obtain reproducible, representative data on the sensory qualities of a food or a glass of water, we use pre-screened panelists in a team because a team is more reliable than a person. The team diminishes the varying influences of individuals.

We tested people who were blind, to see if their sense of smell was better than the average person.[9] What we found is that they became more skillful at smelling. Thus, stop and smell the roses. Take a dog for a walk and follow his lead, smelling as you go. Eat slowly and enjoy the flavor of your food. Be aware of your senses; hone them, exercise them, and let them enhance your life. The more we rely on our sense of smell, the better we get at using it.

But we haven't figured everything out—the senses are intriguing. The multisensory experience of eating and drinking remains a ripe subject for research. And what happens in the brain is an important part of it: memory, emotion, expectation, judgment, and communication. For example, new understanding is changing the way chefs think—changing the study of fine foods or gastronomy. Just look up gastrophysics, molecular gastronomy, and neurogastronomy. New findings are continually being published. It's exciting. It applies to everyday life. It's something my friends and family talk about—sometimes they even listen to me talking about it.

Every human has a smell. A unique
smell. A smell shared with no one else.

~ Molly Birnbaum[1]

Chapter 3
Playing the Detective

WHEN I BROKE INTO THE FIELD OF SMELLING WATER DURING THE mid 1980s, Philadelphia experienced its first recorded bout with geosmin, a nickname for a chemical that smells *earthy*. We had been looking for it for years but it would pop up from time to time, and then leave without a trace. Week after week we would dip a stainless steel bucket into the Schuylkill River to collect water to test for geosmin, or for the microorganisms that emit it. No clues came to us, bucket after bucket.

When the water treatment plant's filters smelled like dry soil—as if I were playing baseball and slid into home base with my face in the dirt—we knew this time we would get some answers. An unusual drought had sucked river flows dangerously low. Customers were calling in and complaining about the smell of the tap water. The river was loaded with a certain type of algae called diatoms. Their skeletons make up diatomaceous earth. But the diatoms were a red herring. Diatoms don't emit geosmin.

On my way home from work I stopped by the treatment plant's

> And there it was—
> the telltale, hair-
> like threads of a
> well-known, smelly
> cyanobacterium.
> Talk about an
> adrenaline rush
> for a water geek!

intake on the river. The clue had to be out there. Maybe it had always been out there and I just had never noticed it before. That happens. Down on the river there were floating clumps of scum. I collected some in a flask and looked at it under the microscope. And there it was—the telltale, hair-like threads of a well-known, smelly cyanobacterium. Talk about an adrenaline rush for a water geek! Cyanobacteria are more commonly called *blue-green algae* but they are technically classified as photosynthetic bacteria. Very high levels of the earthy odor are stored inside their cells so that when the cells burst open, such as when they are subjected to disinfection by chlorine, the geosmin spews out. I kept them in the flask and they grew, winding up the sides of the glass as if they wanted to take over my office.

The cyanobacterium, along with water weeds, were growing in abundance on the river's bottom because the drought allowed sunlight to penetrate deeper into the water—the low flows made the water clearer. Clumps of the earthy smelling lifeform were spread across the sandy-silty bottom, which I could see from a canoe. These bottom growths produced gas bubbles by photosynthesis. The buoyant gassy clumps broke away from the river bottom, rose to the river's surface, and floated downstream accumulating at our plant's intake and in slow moving pools. The deeper green the color of a clump, the more they were filled with bubbles of gas and the geosmin-emitting cyanobacterium.

This was the first recorded appearance of geosmin in Philadelphia. While chemists and engineers, for a long time, had often described our rivers as musty or earthy in smell, they could not test for this natural chemical. They didn't have the laboratory instruments. So who really knows whether this was the *first* appearance? Perhaps it took hold when, during the mid 1900s, the Schuylkill River was dredged of coal residue that had made it toxic. At the same time, federal and state regulations forced everyone to clean up their discharges into the river. The river was now cleaner and healthier—and more favorable for biological growth such as the kind that emits geosmin.

An engineer of a water treatment plant in a small town was beset, unexpectedly, with a severe case of earthy-smelling drinking water caused by geosmin from the lakes from where he got his water. His treatment plant could not handle the onslaught. So he called me for help. I asked, "What are your customers complaining about? Did you actually smell the problem?"

"Yes. It smells earthy," he replied.

I asked, "Does it smell earthy like dry dirt or earthy like moist mulch or earthy like a moldy wine cork?"

The answer was, "Earthy, earthy. I'm not tasting wine, I'm talking about water. I don't know how else to describe it."

By the way, there is another earthy or musty smelling product of cyanobacteria called 2-methylisoborneol, or *MIB* for short. People will tweet, blog, and call in complaints when the water reaches about 10 nanograms per liter. That is a very small amount. MIB is very similar to geosmin. It smells like moist mulch from a flower garden. MIB is a nuisance for coffee makers, but at 100 times the levels found in water because, unlike water which should have no smell, coffee is filled with many aromas that can mask the MIB.[2] Both MIB and geosmin are found worldwide as the two most common odors that plague drinking water supplies. A twin to geosmin that does not occur in water is ethyl fenchol, which smells like fresh moist dirt. While geosmin is hard to synthesize, ethyl fenchol can be made "Kosher" grade. It's hard to imagine that we would want food tasting like dirt.

We wanted to tell our customers that these are natural smells, like rich soil or corn silk. But hold on to your nose! The same cyanobacteria that give off these earthy, musty odors can produce deadly toxins when they form hazardous algal blooms, or *HABs*, that appear as green or reddish colored, oily or stringy films on water. Researchers have claimed that the earthy odors appear at the same place and time as the toxins.[3] These are toxins that can take down a horse in an hour. That's scary! Go ahead and Google "cyanobacteria" and see what you find. So what should we tell our customers when their tap water has a hint of earthy undertones? Is it safe to drink?

This thought takes us to another discipline called risk communication. How do we talk about "safe"? How do we explain complex scientific concepts to the everyday person? One thing is for sure, scientists have trouble explaining to the general public what they know. We use acronyms and scientific terminology that causes confusion. So we hire communication experts to bridge the communication gap. People need to know what we know. They want answers.

People are not the only living beings that smell water. Customers complain when their pets won't drink the tap water because it is earthy. Fish smell water, too.[4] Salmon sense the water in which they were born, remember it, and return to the same water to breed. That's how they find their way home. Unfortunately, pollutants and pesticides can prevent these fish from smelling their way home.

Talking about fish, aquaculture is very important for the world's food supply. But fish take up smells from the water they live in and from the food they eat—smells such as geosmin and MIB. And it's hard to remove these smells. Some scientists cut up the fish into parts and then look for chemicals the fish have taken up from the water. We grab a sample of water from the environment and inject it into a laboratory instrument that will tell us what is in the water. An elderly German fisherman once explained to me how he removes the muddy river flavor from carp. He keeps them alive, takes them home, and stores them in his bathtub for three days before he eats them. The fresh tap water flushes out the river's muddy imprint from the fish.

But there are times when our expensive instruments are of limited help. Instruments cannot smell the way we do. An unusual top note appeared in the water of one of the city's drinking water treatment plants. It was a fleeting whisp of a smell that arose to my nose when I popped off the top of the Erlenmyer flask. If I wasn't ready to smell it right away, it was gone. *Top note* is a term used by wine and perfume experts. It is the highly volatile, initial whiff. Something was in this water that shouldn't be there, but it was hard to describe because it was so fleeting. So there was nothing else to do but follow the trail like a bloodhound tracking down a criminal. No lab instrument was going to help me here.

> So there was nothing else to do but follow the trail like a bloodhound tracking down a criminal. No lab instrument was going to help me here.

We tracked it up a small tributary that had an oil-sheen in the pools along its shoreline. We followed the oil sheen past storm drains and fence line breaks, where people were dumping who-knows-what into the creek at night. Finally we came to a caved-in hole in the ground where the creek ended. The hole looked like a dump. If you let a place pile up with trash, then people will throw trash in it. If it looks like a dump, people will use it like a dump. And sure enough, surveillance subsequently caught someone dumping waste cutting oil into the hole which flowed into the creek and down to our water treatment plant.

Sometimes lab instruments can identify the problem quite readily. Customers complained about a medicinal, chemical smell to their tea and coffee. Back in the lab, with one of our sophisticated analytical instruments, we teased out a volatile chemical called toluene. A can of toluene smells like solvent or paint although what was in the water was at very dilute levels. It was five times greater than its threshold for being able to be smelled but one-twentieth its drinking water standard for health protection. So the water was safe but not pleasant for drinking. When I held a warmed flask of the tainted water to my nose, I thought it was quite okay to drink. The water did not smell bad to me. Two of my co-workers, however, smelled the flask and told me it smelled horrible. For some reason my olfactory system could not pick out toluene from the tap water at that low level. This is not surprising. All of us have smell blindness to certain chemicals, but we likely have no clue about it. This blindness is called specific anosmia, or the inability to detect a certain smell.

Being in the right place at the right time is an important part of solving mysteries. I remember a case regarding newly constructed water pipe. After pipe was installed and approved for use, customers complained about something they had trouble describing. We visited the customers' homes, grabbed samples, and brought the water back to the lab for testing but nothing unusual was found. By the time we got out to the customers and tested their water, it was gone. So what does a detective do? He goes to the scene of the

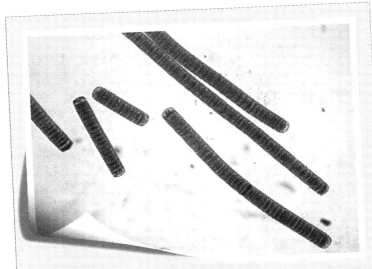

Cyanobacteria make water smell like dry dirt, corn silk, or mulch. They exist worldwide and present a challenge to water treatment managers, increasing the cost of producing a pleasant tasting drinking water.

crime and looks for clues. When I tested the water before it was used by anyone, I found the odor. Our expert noses called it *wet paper*. So I went back to the construction site to look for more clues. I smelled everything that was being used in the construction process from pipe to gaskets to lubricants, and there, in a bucket of what looked like grease from a fast-food dumpster, was the culprit. The cause was the lubricant used on pipe joint gaskets—a vegetable-grease or cheap byproduct from some other industry that made a slippery lubricant. It keeps gaskets from being chewed up when pipes are pushed together.

After a new pipe is installed it is chlorinated to sanitize the inside that will be in contact with the water that people drink. The lube got into the pipe and reacted with the chlorine to form aldehydes that smell like rancid fat and wet paper. The smell accumulated during the night when no one was using water so that in the morning, when the tap water was turned on, the stinky water came out. As we began inspecting new pipe for odors we found as many as half the jobs putting out smelly water, and so we set out to stop it. And that's not the only pipe problem we came across.

Everyone knows that when you put iron in water it gets rusty. Corrosion is a big problem for iron pipe that is buried in the ground. Thus, the outside and inside of the pipe need protection. The inside is lined with cement to protect the metal. Over the cement is a bitumastic or coal tar film to protect the cement. The outside of the pipe can also have a bitumastic coating on it to protect the pipe from the soil. These linings and coatings are made of volatile and semi-volatile organic chemicals such as naphthalene. Curing is when the volatile solvents escape and leave behind a hardened, durable material, like when paint dries. If a bitumastic lining does not cure properly, the water smells like shoe-polish. One pipe had to be flushed for several weeks to remove the smell, because it was not cured before it was loaded with water.

> What else could we do but go in person to her house, sit at her kitchen table, and ask her to give us the water that tasted bad.

Food and beverage producers have long known that packaging affects the quality of their products, from the plastic of water bottles to the lining of soup cans, and the wrappings around food. Metal packaging affects food as well as water. Iron and copper can make water taste like you have a penny in your mouth, *metallic*. But what's interesting is that it's not the same kind of iron that makes water look rusty.[5] It's the form of iron that is usually not seen. And more interesting, it's not a taste. Iron reacts with chemicals in your nasal passageway to create the metallic sensation. It's more like a smell or a nose feel sensation. Copper also gives this metallic sensation but we differ greatly in our sensitivity to it, especially as we get older.[6]

Our plumbing is often made using copper pipe, and sometimes we can smell the copper in the water. A woman kept calling and complaining that her water had an off taste. We collected a sample from her kitchen sink, but nothing showed up when we tested the water in the lab. She insisted that it was not okay. What else could we do but go in person to her house, sit at her kitchen table, and ask her to give us the water that tasted bad. At first we didn't pick anything up. But after tasting a full glass of water we began to get the metallic sensation. Once we could describe what she was tasting, we knew what to test for—metals. Her water had elevated levels of copper and zinc. They came from her plumbing system in her basement; from a maze of plumbing pipes that had been cut and capped and changed over time in ways that trapped sediment and promoted the corrosion of her plumbing.

In another situation, when a restaurant called about its water, we went in person to see what was going on. The water tasted *metallic*, and the customers were complaining. *Ah hah, must be metals again.* We traced the water pipes to a carbonation system for the soda fountain. The pressure from the carbonation system was pushing carbon dioxide back into the water line. The carbonation line was made of plastic. The water line was made of copper. Carbonation chews up copper. And that is what was happening. The carbonation was corroding the copper pipe and loading the water with copper, giving it a metallic flavor.

Unknowingly, a news reporter used water that was affected by copper. He compared city water to other drinking waters in a person-on-the-street taste test. City water failed, or was least preferred. Why? We found that the water that was used to represent city water had a metallic taste. *Ah hah again!* Where did the reporter get his city water for the taste test? From a fountain in the news room. What was in the water? Elevated levels of copper. Where did the copper come from? The building's plumbing.

An alternative to copper is plastic, but plastic has its own issues for the packaging of water. My wife's co-worker complained that his jug of bottled water smelled bad, like gasoline. While there are causes for off flavors in water, gasoline is not usually one of them. Not in Philadelphia. So I asked some questions.

"Where is the water now?" I inquired.

"In my trunk," he replied.

"Do you store it there?" I asked.

"Yes."

"Don't you know that plastic is permeable, and that gasoline odors from your trunk will go right through the plastic bottle and taint the water inside?" I said.

"I guess I never thought of that," he said.

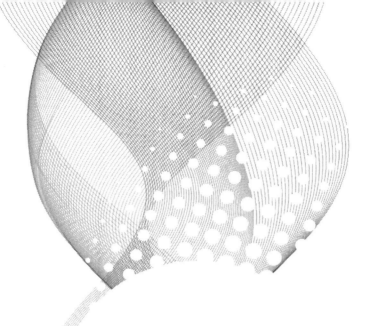

In the space of a few years they had drawn up a table of respirable "airs" and stinking emanations. It was a confused, tangled classification, and the terminology was still ambiguous.

~ Alain Corbin[1]

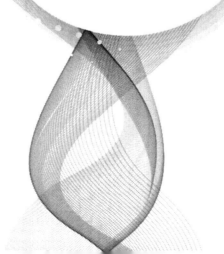

Chapter 4

Making Connections

Put me in a room with an intimate gathering and I will find a corner to hide in—at least until I find someone to connect with; until I hear someone talk about water, or the senses, or something that I am passionate about. Then you won't be able to shut me up. We gravitate toward people we have something in common with. We connect with people we would otherwise never have connected with, all because we share something - an interest, an experience, a passion, a dream.

I arranged a beer tasting challenge for a friend's 40th birthday. I lined up ten different popular beers in colored plastic cups—so no one could cheat by using visual cues—and warmed them to room temperature. A beer's aroma is more noticeable when it is warm. (Yet Americans prefer ice cold beer!) I arranged them in order from non-alcoholic to bitter stout. I gave each guest ten cards with the names of the different beers; they had to match the names to the right cups by tasting and smelling. The best anyone could do was get three correct, with two being the obvious bookends of the non-alcoholic and the stout. One guest could not identify her favorite brand, which was the only brand she would drink. We tend to think we are more knowledgeable and discerning than we really are about the food we eat and the beverages we drink.

Good beer depends in large part on the chemistry and flavor of its water.[2] Chlorine, rust, copper, geosmin, and MIB need to be removed before the water is used in brewing. Yet, not everything in water is a problem for beer. To the contrary, some natural ingredients of water are necessary for brewing. The biology and chemistry of brewing requires certain ranges of alkalinity, pH or acidity, and calcium. Chloride and sulfate are also useful. The flavor of beer depends in part on the ingredients of the water used to make it.

> I had an opportunity to carry on that tradition as a master brewer or beer executive. I was an intern at the time in the quality control laboratory of a brewery, getting doused in beer while collecting samples from the keg filler.

William Penn, as Philadelphia's founder, made sure that he had a brew house for his own use, and that the people of his city had access to beer. It was safer than the water, as well as nourishing and spirit-lifting. I had an opportunity to carry on that tradition as a master brewer or beer executive. I was an intern at the time in the quality control laboratory of a brewery, getting doused in beer while collecting samples from the keg filler. But that was when beer in Philadelphia was on its way out, before microbreweries came into fashion. So I turned down the opportunity and chose water instead.

Back in the 1700s, chemists described and classified odors. A survey of the river Seine, during 1790, sleuthed out the poisonous stench of the river in its banks of black mud.[3] These chemists dared to smell cesspools that caused mortalities. They dared to explore the world around them at a time in history when the sense of smell was considered useful only to animals, not fit for the healthy development of intellectuals. But they didn't have the laboratory instruments that we have today to test the water, so they did the best they could with what they had.

One hundred years ago, the degree of water pollution was tested by shaking a half-filled bottle until the water foamed like a head of beer.[4] A stable foam translated to heavy organic pollution. Then based on its smell, it would be examined under the microscope. As for tasting, it was considered of little value because most problems in water were caused by bad smells.

Another test that was used to evaluate the degree of pollution was the Putrescibility Test.[5] Take a bottle of water, plug it with a stopper, and let it sit at room temperature for a few days. If the water turns black and has a "putrefactive" smell then it is "putrescible" or unfit for use.

Yet another standardized water test[6] looked for the odors that signify decomposing organic matter, plankton, and industrial wastes. Smelling made sense. Clearly at this time in history, the human nose was more sensitive than any laboratory instrument. Waters were smelled at room temperature and again at a higher temperature to tease out the volatile odors. Daring and curious noses described the smells as aromatic like cloves, balsamic, flowery, chemical, disagreeable, earthy, grassy, musty like a damp cellar, or smelling like vegetables.

Such chemists described Philadelphia's rivers as smelling like decaying vegetation. What else was in the rivers one hundred years ago but leaves and grass! Take grass and place it in water and let it decay. At first it smells like grassy water. Grass that is cut emits green leaf volatiles that birds sense to locate places where insects are easily found. These chemicals that give grass its fresh green smell are useful inside a cow's gut where they help produce milk for drinking and for making cheese.[7] But after a day or two, the grass in water smells like decaying grass, a little septic. And after several more days it is quite septic. This progression is largely due to the formation of organic sulfides. Natural decay produces a soup of sulfides that vary in concentration depending on how long the decay has progressed.

We spent considerable effort developing an understanding of which container to use for smelling and tasting water, and at what temperature to serve it. All of this research was to get the most from the human sensory system, in a reproducible way, to dissect the flavor of water.

There was an attempt to standardize such descriptions of how water smells such as those caused by organic matter and by living organisms, and those caused by chlorine to treat water.[8] The odors that water emitted were classified as aromatic, cucumber, chlorine, earthy, fishy, grassy, geranium, medicinal, musk-melon, moldy, musty, nasturtium, oily, pigpen, sweetish, hydrogen sulfide, vegetable, and violet. A rating scale was also developed to record how strong each smell was, from not perceptible, to very faint, to very strong wherein the water was unfit to drink.

But this was not good enough. With our sense of smell being the most sensitive instrument available for evaluating water, we pushed the nose to its limits. The threshold at which water just begins to smell was considered something to measure. To this end, the osmoscope was developed.[9] It was described by the Chicago Daily Tribune (January 8, 1934) as a mechanical nose that magnified the sense of smell of the headspace air in a laboratory flask of warmed water. The scope had one end of a glass tube extended through a stopper into a flask's headspace. The other end had two nostril pieces to stick up the nose.

> With our sense of smell being the most sensitive instrument available for evaluating water, we pushed the nose to its limits. The threshold at which water just begins to smell was considered something to measure.

This was followed by the desire to detect the threshold, or point at which water no longer smelled, derived from its dilution. If the whole smell experience could be distilled down to a single number then scientists and engineers had something easier to work with.

This number was called the threshold odor number. When it exceeds a level of three, the water is unacceptable. But the way water smells is more complicated than that. And as a result, research into the methods for smelling water stagnated for decades.

Picking a number that should not be exceeded for a chemical in water so that the water never smells bad is quite hard to do. A very public attempt to limit the level at which a chemical causes water to smell involved methyl tertiary butyl ether, or MtBE. It's a gasoline additive. When underground gasoline storage tanks leaked, MtBE contaminated the groundwater wells. People should not have it in their water, let alone smell it. But setting a number that tells us when people will not smell it has been very difficult. In fact, because of the complexity of our sensory systems, there is no single number. Your number will be different than mine, and my number will be different from day to day, from morning to night. Determining a level at which water will never smell has been a difficult task to accomplish and so the debate, even in the court of law, has gone on for years.

For decades now we have taken up the battle to secure clean drinking water for the majority of people living in the USA. We want to be able to confidently say that our public water is safe to drink. But we don't go so far as to claim that the tap water is health enhancing. We talk about the absence of contaminants that could negatively affect your health rather than the presence of ingredients that promote your health. We talk about water not having any bad taste or smell—it should be pure tasting and free of objections.

In the 1970s, the US Environmental Protection Agency set national standards for drinking water, and these included standards for the aesthetic quality. These aesthetic standards are called Secondary Maximum Contaminant Levels because they are not primary health standards but guidelines on the aesthetic properties of water. If the taste, odor, color, or temperature of tap water is unacceptable for a water utility's customers then they could make bad choices; they could turn to unsafe water, or they could vote against actions to secure safer water.[10,11,12,13,14,15] So the EPA set guidelines for copper, iron, zinc, manganese, chloride, and other chemicals as well as the color and odor of water.

When you hang out with the experts, you learn the tricks of the trade. There are many tricks used in sensory studies because the measuring instrument is the human sensory system, which is connected to the human brain. Some tricks are based on chemistry. Others rely on perceptions, expectations, and past experiences.

The colder something is, the less volatile the aroma will be. The less volatile, the less we smell. And so we suggest that water consumers fill a pitcher, place it in the refrigerator, and drink it cold. The chlorine smell will be less noticeable at the cold temperature. But for beer and wine it's a different story. You lose the fullness of their flavors when you drink them right out of the refrigerator.

There's a trick that fragrance chemists use to pull apart the components of a perfume. It's not based on chemistry but rather on how the brain works. If you sniff a specific aroma, such as in a perfume, at a high concentration, or strong intensity, you will blank out your ability to smell it for a short time. Then you can go back and sniff the perfume to smell the other notes that were hiding beneath the one you blanked out. You can pull apart a perfume and recreate its recipe. If you ever painted a room in your house you might recall that, after about an hour, you stopped noticing the new paint smell. But when you took a sip from your cup of coffee, you had no problem smelling the aroma of the coffee.

Deodorizers employ some of these tactics. They can tie up or chemically change the smell in the air that we inhale through our noses. Or they can mask the nuisance odor, hiding it from our brains. These deodorizers are used in bathrooms. They are also used at waste treatment plants. I remember one that smelled like the barbershop I went to when I was a kid. The barber gave me bubble gum after my haircut was done if I sat still for the cut. The waste's masking agent smelled like bubble gum in an attempt to fool the brain into only noticing the bubble gum scent.

> A fun way to fool the brain is to change the color of your food or drink. Would pink colored celery, purple bananas, or green colored orange juice still taste the same?

A fun way to fool the brain is to change the color of your food or drink. Would pink colored celery, purple bananas, or green colored orange juice still taste the same? A white wine, dyed red, can fool your brain to think it's red wine instead. If I placed three cups of water before you, and they were colored red, blue, and transparent, you would likely associate the red cup with a rusty flavored water because everyone knows that rust is red in color.

Since our sensory systems are connected to our brains, it is very important how you ask a question when doing a study—it affects the answer you get from the human attached to the nose or tongue. Have you ever been paid for participating in a focus group? The facilitator can easily influence the group by the way the questions are phrased and by the order in which they are asked. Consumer studies on tasting need to be very carefully designed so as not to bias the human subjects and get bad information on which wrong decisions would be made. The nose is connected to a brain which is part of a human, and all of this must be considered when using people as smelling and tasting instruments. This makes it much harder to measure smells and tastes than measuring a chemical or temperature, but it also makes it more interesting and challenging.

The science of water has benefited from advancements made in the food industry. The sensory analysis of food came into its own during the first half of the 20th century.[16] Food preservation, quality control, and product development were made possible in part by the development of reproducible techniques to taste and smell food. Psychologists looked at sensory perceptions, connecting smells with emotions while psychophysical scientists linked the subjective sensory experience to physical properties, or the chemical makeup of food. This era of sensory research produced an explosion of food R&D that can now be seen in the vast array of food products and brands that line grocery store shelves. While the sensory qualities of food drove multi-million dollar decisions, tap water was based on a take it or leave it basis: If it smells bad today, tough. Nothing we can do about it!

I joined a group of water companies from California, Pennsylvania, Spain, and France that began training their laboratory people to be water tasters and smellers using a technique developed by Arthur D. Little, Inc., called the flavor profile method.[17] In flavor profiling, highly trained assessors dissect the flavor of a food or beverage, such as water, into its component tastes and smells to form a profile. A glass of tap water might be broken down into a moderately strong chlorinous smell with a hint of a barely noticeable mustiness, and a very slight, drying mouth feel. The profile does not tell you if the water is good or bad. It makes no judgment on preference or acceptance. It simply tells you what sensory notes combine to construct its overall flavor.

With this new tool, teams of scientists tasted and smelled water, and described its sensory profile characteristics. From different countries with different waters, a common list of tastes and smells was captured in what is called a flavor wheel. Flavor wheels are used to describe wine, beer, coffee, fish, and so on. Search the Internet using "flavor wheel" or "odor wheel" and the product you are interested in such as cheese, catfish, or olive oil. With flavor wheels you can learn the language of the sensory snobs.

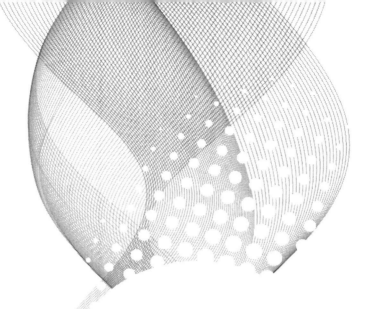

So closely is sniffing tied to odor perception that people routinely sniff when they are asked to imagine a smell. Without prompting, they take larger sniffs when imagining pleasant odors and smaller ones when imagining malodors.

~ Avery Gilbert[1]

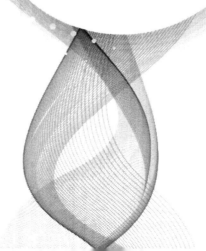

Chapter 5

Taking a Detour

THE DRINKING WATER PROFESSION HAS ENGINEERS BY THE BOAT LOAD, along with chemists, biologists, customer service inspectors, information technologists, administrative and financial officers, manufacturers, contractors, regulators, board members, and commissioners. There is no position, though, with responsibility for the aesthetic quality of water. In the perfume or fragrance business they call the sensory expert *the nose*. In the culinary arts, this is the executive chef or *chef de cuisine*. Those who mix and match food flavors are called *flavorists*. When it comes to wine, we have the *sommelier*, and with beer we have the *professional beer taster*. With tea it might be *tea master*. There is even a *salt master*; an expert salt taster for the wide selection of novel salts: salts with different grain sizes and colors; salt that is smoked or spiced; salt from the mines or from the sea. *Master water taster* or *professional water taster* or *water master* is not on any company's employee list. Apparently you can obtain a certificate from Germany as a trained *mineral water sommelier*. *Master sewage sniffer*, or *sewage master* could apply to some of us, too, but you won't see that on our business cards.

Since I was an expert tap water taster, it seemed only logical to apply my skills to the smell of waste. All I had known about the smell of waste was in distinguishing the garbage from the trash. Household paper, plastic, and metal waste is *trash*. *Garbage* was what we called the food waste that country people tossed into compost piles. My dad put out garbage in a small pail. Farmers' trucks collected it as food for their pigs. Garbage days were stinky, especially during the summer. But this was acceptable. However, if you lived downwind of a sewage treatment plant, that was a different story.

A hunter understands wind direction because if a deer is downwind of the hunter, it won't be there long. That's because we stink. But city folk can't tell which way the wind is blowing. Neighborhood residents have complained about the smell of a sewage plant when the wind was not even blowing the smell in their direction. If you follow the wind, you follow the track of the odors. If you are considering building a house near a sewage plant, make sure you check the prevailing wind direction.

Convection can help reduce those stinky sewage odors. Convection is the rising of warm air, as in a hot air balloon. On a hot sunny day, the ground heats up the air, which rises straight up into the sky. For a sewage plant this is a good thing. It carries the odors high into the atmosphere, above the community where only the birds can smell it. But developers still build housing developments downwind of sewage treatment plants. And the plants become the targets for residents who don't like the smell. Empowered by today's environmental awareness, the people of the communities protest. But what can we do? Move the sewage plant to a different location, or place a huge bubble over it to contain the odors? I got roped into studying sewage odors for this very reason.

If you think that castle moats were bucolic waterways that circled picturesque castles, think again. The deadly stench of the moat may have been the best defense against intruders. Where do you think all the castle waste went? As people settled in deserts and on mountains, along rivers and below glaciers, they found ways to dispose of their waste, and the closest water body was always a top choice. That is, once the waste was taken out of the home it had to go somewhere. But inside the home, long ago, families kept pots in which to collect their urine to sell to tanneries that used it to treat animal skins. Today we simply flush the toilet and it's gone. Imagine keeping chamber pots under your bed at night!

During the late 1800s, human waste was collected in privy pits and cesspools beneath houses, or in the back yards, or in the streets. You could report your neighbor to the board of health if his pit was overflowing. Privy cleaners and night soil men had the glorious task of taking this waste away and selling it to farmers. After the Civil War ended in the United States, indoor water closets replaced outhouses and became the common means by which to accumulate all the waste, causing more intense and frequent problems until they were hooked up to underground brick sewers that moved the waste away from the houses.

The ancient Romans had a large sewer they called *Cloaca Maxima*. They appreciated the need to control water in all its

> Throughout history there have been swings in opinion as to whether our solid and liquid waste can be put to good use, or whether it's just plain dangerous, even evil.

various forms; to keep it from stagnating in the city. One of their gods was called *Sterculius*. He was the first to lay dung upon the earth, and so he was their god of fertilization. How about worshipping this god? Those Romans were flush with good ideas!

Waste was not always considered something that needed to be out of sight and out of smell. Throughout history there have been swings in opinion as to whether our solid and liquid waste can be put to good use, or whether it's just plain dangerous, even evil.[2] Cultures arose that believed that human waste could restore youth, protect us against infections, and clean and purify. It was not linked to disease. Can you believe that?

If you think sewage stinks, let it stagnate for an hour and it really gets cooking. It will knock your socks off. We say that the sewage is no longer *fresh*. The main reason for this is the loss of oxygen. When all the oxygen is used up, the bacteria that grow in the absence of oxygen make obnoxious odors of decay.

Nitrogen-based and sulfur-based smelly chemicals in domestic sewage come from amino acids and proteins: they are what we eat. Nitrogen-based chemicals include ammonia and amines. Sulfur-based chemicals include hydrogen sulfide and other organic sulfides. Hydrogen sulfide gives the signature rotten-egg odor. Hydrogen sulfide can be deadly. If you stand in the presence of high levels of hydrogen sulfide, the rotten-egg odor will seem to disappear in minutes. The problem is, it has not gone away; your sensory system and brain have stopped telling you it is there. If you don't understand this, you could be dead in minutes. You may think the air is safe to breathe, and then you are unconscious. Nonetheless, hydrogen sulfide is also essential to our health.

Hydrogen sulfide in our blood stream helps control inflammation in our bodies.[3] The folk lore on the benefits of eating garlic might be true. Sulfur odors are an important component of foods and beverages, and so they abound in the stuff we ingest as well as the waste we excrete. Sulfur chemicals (hydrogen sulfide, dimethyl sulfide, and many other sulfur-based chemicals) come from garlic, cabbage, broccoli, and cauliflower. Also included are aldehydes with their green, vegetable, and rancid smells.[4] While these *mal*-odors produce psychological effects, such as headaches and nausea when they are associated with sewage, many of them exist in cooked meats and fish, fruits, vegetables, coffee, beer, wine, and cheese. We object to these smells when we live downwind of a sewage treatment plant, but we relish them in the foods we eat.

People are curious about stinks. We don't usually admit it, but bad odors draw us in. There is a flower that makes smelling sewage a pleasant experience. It's known as the Corpse Flower, a giant plant from Indonesia that blooms once every ten years. And it is a good thing that it takes so long to bloom, for the flower gives off a rotting, putrid smell that attracts flies and beetles. The smell also attracts curious people.

Stinks surround us in everyday life and often go unnoticed until someone draws them to our attention. Scientists now know why dirty clothes smell the way they do. The odor is produced by a bacterium.[5] The sweaty odor is due to the chemical 4-methyl-3-hexenoic acid, a fatty acid present in underarm sweat. Your clothes can smell that way, too, and it is hard to wash out. Your bath towels, pillow cases, and socks can also absorb this odor.

We emit stinky odors when we breathe. Scientists have found that bad breath is composed of volatile organic chemicals including hydrogen sulfide, methyl mercaptan, and dimethyl sulfide. And that the smell of poop is due to sulfur chemicals. Even studies of farts have found similar chemistry at play. Babies who are fed store bought milk and soy formula, instead of breast milk, produce more of these stinky chemicals.[6] Stench is all around us, a part of normal everyday life.

I became an expert at sniffing the air downwind of a wastewater treatment plant, naming and recording the various types of malodors that crossed the fence line. Imagine walking into public bathrooms, and sniffing and recording the aromas! I found that while hydrogen sulfide could be detected inside the sewage plant, it was not escaping into the community and causing a nuisance. However, other odors were traveling on the wind, through people's open windows, and invading their bedrooms at night.[7] And there was, at the time, no easy way to detect and monitor these nuisances except by using the human nose. So I spent hours, with co-workers, walking around the fence line of the wastewater plant getting intimately familiar with its smells, training my nose as a master sewage sniffer.

> I became an expert at sniffing the air downwind of a wastewater treatment plant, naming and recording the various types of malodors that crossed the fence line.

The liquid part of sewage gets sanitized and treated before it's sent back into the water cycle. Well-treated wastewater, after it has been fully treated and disinfected, should smell like a marsh. The sludge, or all the junk that settles to the bottom (nasty stuff that can begin to stink in minutes) gets further processed for beneficial uses such as the formation of methane which can then be burned to gen-

The human nose is a powerful instrument. It can be highly trained to distinguish taints in water at picograms per liter. It can also be used to determine if the processes in a wastewater treatment plant are operating as designed.

erate electricity. The scum, that floating debris of corn kernels, condoms, and grease (visually nasty stuff) gets collected and sent off for incineration or landfilling. Believe it or not, I spent time separating all three phases of wastewater so I could smell each one. That is what a scientist does, out of curiosity.

And the smells were different. I found that a fast-food restaurant's dumpster can smell like scum because of the fats and grease, including butyric acid that adds to the flavor of cheese and the smell of the ginkgo tree; a hardy Asian tree, so hardy it survived Hiroshima. The female ginkgo releases fleshy seeds that smash on sidewalks and stink up neighborhoods. Cities have tried to plant only male trees but sometimes these trees change gender, and develop stinky seeds just out of spite.

Every serious kitchen has a spice rack: cinnamon, curry, black pepper, celery, parsley, thyme, and various types of salt. Spices add flavors to food. Back in the laboratory we have our spice rack, too —vials of pure chemicals with which to train instruments to recognize wastewater. Amines emit fishy odors. Carboxylic acids have rancid odors. Organic sulfides produce skunky and cabbagy odors. Mercaptans, dead animal. Terpenes, woody. And geosmin, the earthy odor. Like a bird watcher who collects a lifetime list of bird sightings, I added to my lifetime list of smells: barny, dead crab, burnt coffee, ammoniacal, fecal, detergenty, briny, oniony, and many others.

Stench can tingle your eyes and nose. When you cut into an onion, for example, you release the sulfur chemicals that react with enzymes from cutting the onion to volatilize the chemicals that get into your eyes and dissolve in the water to produce an irritation due to sulfuric acid, sulfur dioxide, and hydrogen sulfide.[8] Thus, you cry. Ammonia and bleach tingle your nose. If you lose your sense of smell, you may still detect them by their nose-feel sensations.

Digesters hold wastewater sludge until it decays and becomes stable enough for beneficial uses. But digester gas, or the bacterial burps that collect in the headspace of the tanks, can escape and stink up a neighborhood. I remember lying in bed one night, after a day of walking across the roof of digesters, still getting whiffs of digester gas. The window was closed. I didn't live downwind of a sewage plant. So where was that smell coming from? Did you ever smell your hair after hanging around a campfire—it will smell of wood smoke. Hair is a good absorbent of odors—in fact, perfume should be sprayed on hair rather than on skin. The ancient Egyptians poured and melted perfume over their hair. And hairy bodies are smellier bodies. The obnoxious digester gas had absorbed onto my mustache. Now some of the chemicals that make sewage stink can be sexually attractive to men. At very low levels, the fecal smell drawn from the civet, a nocturnal Ethiopian cat, can be mixed into perfume to attract men.[9] Men find low levels of fecal smells to be sexually attractive. Nevertheless, since the smelly mustache was located just under my nose, I shaved it off.

Other smells bring to mind summer vacations. When I drive to the shore for a day at the beach, I know when I am getting close because I can start to detect the smell of the marsh. A sulfur chemical that contributes to the smell of the sea is dimethyl sulfide, or DMS for short.[10] That lovely smell of the sea, spiced with salt, is an important part of the natural cycling of sulfur by phytoplankton or whale food. But DMS is also an important flavorant in beer, coffee, cabbage, cheese, and wine. And this same DMS caused a nuisance odor at one of my city's wastewater treatment plants. I called it canned corn—though not all canned corn smells this way. It reminded me of the large, yellow kernel corn of a generic supermarket brand. This canned corn odor escaped the sewage plant and traveled on the wind into the neighboring community. It took a decade to track this chemical's source to the breakdown of a harmless but very useful household product that was being dumped into the sewer system by one industrial plant.

Long before I was born, people believed that smells could protect them from the deadly plague that ravaged Europe. While the plague was not caused by bad smells, plague victims emitted a stench.[11] So people burned, scented, and deodorized whatever they could to offset bad odors which they thought were carrying the disease—even to the extent of smelling their own privy waste. I know what waste smells like; so please give me a scented candle instead!

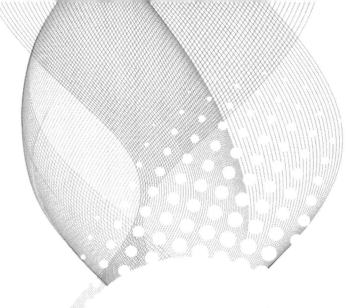

Each day, we breathe about 23,040 times and move around 438 cubic feet of air. It takes us about five seconds to breathe—two seconds to inhale and three seconds to exhale—and, in that time, molecules of odor flood through our systems.

~ Diane Ackerman[1]

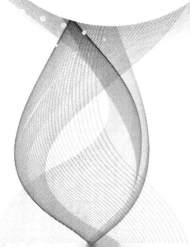

Chapter 6
Telling Stories

Whe you know someone intimately, you know the color of their hair and the appearance of their face; you know the sound of their voice and the touch of their hands. Facial images, fingerprints, eyes, and even odor prints uniquely identify us. Yet if our senses are so important for establishing intimate relationships with one another then why do we hide behind fragranced soap, hand gel, cologne, deodorants, and perfume? Why do we scent our bodies, color our hair, and wear contact lenses? Think about it. Your mother's natural, unique smell was important to you when you were a baby. You find comfort in the scent of your lover's clothing or pillow.

We connect with each other through our senses while at the same time hiding from each other. The air space between us is loaded with chemicals, some that smell and some that don't smell.[2] More than 700 chemicals can be detected in the air between us. Such chemicals include the odor of biscuit or 4-heptenal; of hazelnut or filbertone; of paper or 2-nonenal; of tar or naphthalene; and,

> Think about it. Your mother's natural, unique smell was important to you when you were a baby. You find comfort in the scent of your lover's clothing or pillow.

of urine or benzoic acid. Some of the chemicals between us cause repulsion while others cause attraction. This is where the magical pheromones come into play.[3] Although scientists have yet to prove their existence for humans, the manufacturers of perfume, cologne, and other products invest large sums of money into a belief in pheromones.

Diet, health, and genetics drive the types of chemicals we exude into the air around us. We emit different odors based on whether we are meat eaters or vegetarians, the amount of apocrine glands in our skin, and how much hair we have on our bodies.[4] And when we get sick, we emit other odors. Doctors were once trained to recognize diseases by the smells from sick people. Typhus smells like mice. Diabetes like fruit. Measles like freshly plucked bird feathers. Yellow fever smells like a butcher's shop, and kidney failure like ammonia.

So if all of these odors are due to chemicals, then why don't we just measure the chemicals? Because it's not that easy to do! Let's take water as an example; a gas chromatograph tied to a mass spectrometer can detect over two hundred chemicals in one glass of musty-smelling water. But there are only about a dozen chemicals that produce the smell of water, and they occur at concentrations as low as a nanogram or picogram per liter. A nanogram per liter, or part per trillion, is equivalent to three seconds in a hundred thousand years.

We once tried to merge the human nose with the laboratory instrument to dissect the odors of water.[5] We put a chemist's nose on the end of a gas chromatograph so we could match what the nose smelled to the chemicals being detected by the instrument. Lots of potentially smelly chemicals came out that did not match the smell of the water in the glass.

Throughout the 1980s there would be brief periods of time when upwards of three hundred customer complaints would come in over the phone during only a few days. Lab testing could find no reasons for the complaints. The water's chemistry was normal. The biology was normal. No industrial spills were reported. But our trained flavor profilers called the problem cucumber-like in its flavor. Imagine tap water smelling like a sliced cucumber. Pepsi once released a new product in a green bottle, in Japan, called *Pepsi Ice Cucumber*. The flavor was supposed to enhance the cooling sensation of Pepsi and make it a more desirable summertime beverage.[6] I don't know if it ever worked, but tap water with a cucumber flavor? I can't see that ever working.

> But our trained flavor profilers called the problem cucumber-like in its flavor. Imagine tap water smelling like a sliced cucumber.

I challenged a team of high school students with a vial containing the cucumber odor, but they were not told what it was except that it was an odor that could occur in tap water. As a team, they agreed to tell me that it smelled chlorine-like or chemical-like. One student said it smelled like a cucumber but the rest of the group told him that didn't make sense. *Water doesn't smell like a cucumber.*

People will try to make logical associations with what they think should give water an off flavor: *chemical*, *chlorine*, and *metallic*. Yet we could train them to recognize the cucumber smell. We trained our treatment plant operators to recognize the flavor by sniffing sliced cucumbers. Since the water treatment plants are manned around the clock to monitor the operating processes, the operators test the water around the clock. This includes sniffing for odors.

Back in the lab, now that we knew the correct description of the problem, we could search the scientific literature for clues. An article from an agriculture research journal reported that scientists were studying the chemicals that make fruits and vegetables smell the way they do. They had found that cucumbers and melons have certain chemicals associated with their flavor. So we purchased the chemicals and began sniffing them. One particular chemical—trans-2,cis-6 nonadienal—matched the flavor we were looking for. It had been described as early as 1939 and was confirmed using advanced instrumentation in 1990.[7] We tossed out the cucumber slices and trained our team to recognize the actual cucumber's chemical.

Then after years of watching and waiting, during a warm, rainy February the cucumber flavor returned to our water and stayed for a month. We drove up the Delaware River, which is the source for the affected treatment plant, smelling its tributaries. It took several trips over two weeks to progressively sample and sniff the various waters upstream. When we came to a fork in the river between the East and West branches, the East Branch smelled musty but the West Branch smelled like cucumber, and it was so strong I could smell it in the stainless steel sample collection bucket as I heaved it up onto the bridge. Up the West Branch we went until, standing below the spillway of a large water supply reservoir I could smell the cucumber fragrance in the air. I was very excited that I had found the source of the cucumber smell after so many years. Some aroma companies claim that the smell of a cucumber increases one's libido. Perhaps that is why the fragrance laces many personal bathing products.

It was an overcast day and fairly warm for that time of year. It was perfect weather for smelling because such weather keeps the odors close to the ground. The spillway was overflowing because the ice-covered reservoir was full. Microorganisms were growing under the protection of the ice, living off the nutrients from upstream dairy farms. The reservoir was spilling the microorganisms and their smell into the Delaware River. So we grabbed some samples and headed home. Back in the lab we found that the very chemical that gives cucumber its flavor was the chemical produced by the microorganisms in the reservoir way upriver.

Why did this cause us problems over 200 miles downstream? When the US Environmental Protection Agency was formed during the 1970s it was looking for chemicals to regulate. That's what regulators do! At the same time, researchers uncovered chemical byproducts of drinking water chlorination. That's what researchers do! One was the chemical chloroform, which has its own interesting history.

Dr. Samuel Guthrie discovered chloroform back in the 1830s. In those days he described it by its taste and smell, and its intoxicating effects. It had a nice pleasant flavor, sweet and aromatic. People would drink it, as it was better than alcohol. About ten years later it became known as an anesthetic, which was greatly needed in the days when it was all too common to amputate infected legs and arms. Today, chloroform is a major chlorination byproduct and a carcinogen. It is lumped into a group of chemicals called trihalomethanes or THMs. When natural water is hit with chlorine

Water is vital to life. We must value it and protect it, especially since it is a limited resource. Every drop of water that travels through the water cycle is important, whether it falls with the rain or travels through the sewer.

to kill the pathogens that cause cholera and typhoid, the chlorine reacts with natural organic matter from decaying leaves and grass. This reaction produces THMs. Water utilities, such as ours in Philadelphia, were forced to deal with these chlorination byproducts. No longer could we overload the water with chlorine. We had to change our practices.

First, we reduced the amount of chlorine we added up front in the treatment process to feed it progressively in smaller amounts throughout the process until the water was eventually treated. Second, we added ammonia after treatment was all done to tie up the leftover chlorine into what's known as *chloramine*. One outcome, though, was a reduction in the treatment power of chlorine. This meant that the cucumber flavor could break through and get into the drinking water. Today we call this an *unintended consequence* —or, when I try to fix one thing I break something else. The water treatment plants upriver from Philadelphia reported no unusual flavor to their drinking water because they were still dumping plenty of chlorine into their water. So we had to switch to something other than chlorine. Potassium permanganate, a chemical that gives water a purple color, turned out to be a good solution. It did not produce chlorination byproducts and it removed the cucumber flavor upfront in the process without affecting the drinking water.

Water utilities, such as ours in Philadelphia, were forced to deal with these chlorination byproducts. No longer could we overload the water with chlorine. We had to change our practices.

Throughout history, people have preferred good tasting water even when it was not safe to consume. When chlorine was introduced to drinking water for safety, many people returned to spring water that was not safe. This connection between how water tastes and smells hinders our attempts, worldwide, to stop infant mortality due to waterborne diseases. People still use their senses to support their preference for the water they drink.[8]

The hint of a smell of chlorine in tap water, to me, suggests a safer

The hint of a smell of chlorine in tap water, to me, suggests a safer water. But this is not so to many other people in the world.

water. But this is not so to many other people in the world. In some countries, the smell of chlorine might mean something went wrong. Or the smell of chlorine might be rejected altogether with a preference for boiling water and drinking it warm. There's a complex relationship between people's experience with water and what they are willing to pay for clean water. For example, the more water that people use, the less they tend to value it.[9] And if they don't value it, they will not support advancements in science and engineering that make it safer.

Water is a global issue, and the need for scientists and engineers to commit to careers in water is never ending. There are problems yet to be solved, research waiting to be done, changes waiting to take place. Whether you are in Asia or Europe, Africa or the Caribbean, water is important and vital to everyone's personal health as well as to every community's well-being. Travel the world and come to your own conclusion—water is a global issue.

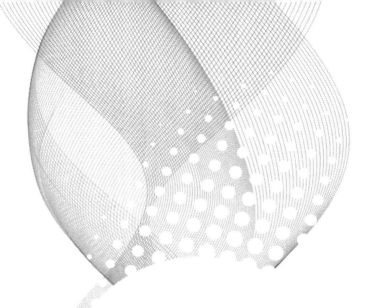

We keep an eye out for wonders, my daughter and I, every morning as we walk down our farm lane to meet the school bus. And wherever we find them they reflect the magic of water: a spider web drooping with dew like a rhinestone necklace.

~ Barbara Kingsolver[1]

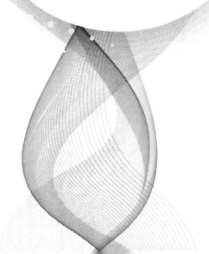

Chapter 7
Testing the Waters

D ID YOU EVER DRINK THE RAIN WATER RIGHT OUT OF THE SKY? HOW did it taste? I don't remember rain water having a taste. Yet when a storm approaches, the air begins to smell. To me the smell of rain is not a description but a memory. The smell of a coming storm can transport me back to a hot summer day, sitting beneath a canvas awning stretched out over the patio of my red brick row house, layers of clouds moving in opposite directions, and far-off boomers inciting boyhood fascinations of cannon and infantry charges.

Scientists have confirmed that the coming rain does smell. In 1964, mineralogists Isabel Joy Bear and R.G. Thomas named this smell *petrichor*. It is the vapors rising off stone or dry natural earth when the atmosphere changes due to an approaching storm.[2] The moisture in the air along with the drop in barometric pressure unravels dried animal and plant matter clinging to rock, concrete, and asphalt. Sniff abundantly. You might smell the earthy, musty odors of soil and compost, the green smell of grass, or the dusty smell of hot cement. The coming storm pushes before it a curtain of smell which incites a lifetime of memories.

Then the rain comes. And rain water may not have a good smell to it. Especially the first flush that brings with it the polluted atmosphere. In the cities of the late 1800s, the air was so filled with soot that the rain washed it out of the sky. City rain was different from country rain, which was purer.[3] When rain drops evaporated they left a dark brown, varnish-smelling residue.[4] Snow was no different. Even before it hit the ground it turned yellow as it carried the atmospheric pollution with it.

What about ice? When it forms, does it squeeze out all impurities so that what is left is pure, frozen H_2O? If you travel to countries where the water is unsafe to drink, you do not want ice in your boiled water. Ice can carry germs with it. When disease busters investigate a waterborne disease outbreak they will collect ice because ice preserves the evidence that may have come and gone before they could get to the scene. And when a glass of water smells fishy, it may not be the water but the ice. The ice in your freezer is a good absorber of odors such as from fish fillets. This is nothing new. Back in the late 1800s when ice was harvested from the frozen waterways, polluted rivers produced bad ice. The scientists couldn't explain it, but it looked and tasted bad.

Ice floats on water. If it didn't, much of the life on earth would have died a long time ago. But floating ice puts a cap on pollution and keeps it from being released. In 1875, a *Report of the Water Supply for the City of Philadelphia* by its Commission of Engineers argued that in winter the ice should be harvested from the Schuylkill River to allow for aeration which would reduce the offensive odors caused by decaying organic matter: *If this were done, we think that every citizen of Philadelphia might be thankful if he could always enjoy as healthful and refreshing a beverage as Fairmount water, cooled in summer by Fairmount ice.* The report went on to say, *It is further known that it is not so much the quantity, as the nature or condition of the dissolved organic matter, that deter-mines the goodness or badness of a water used as a beverage. Ten grains of dry putrescible sewage matter in a gallon might prove dele-terious, while one hundred grains or more of tea or coffee in a gallon are most welcome, refreshing and healthful.*

Putting ice in a glass of water is largely an American preference. But if you pay a high price for a bottle of mineral water in a restau-rant, the last thing you want to do is drop in some ice cubes made with tap water. You will be diluting out the mineral water's flavor.

Good tasting water is judged by comparison to your spit, which constantly bathes the taste buds in your mouth. Yes, here we go again with spit. It contains sodium, chloride, calcium, bicarbonate, phos-phate, potassium, and magnesium—similar to good mineral water. And temperature and acidity help determine how these chemicals behave in your mouth. Water that has been treated to be extra pure and free of these minerals no longer has the recipe for being good tasting, and so minerals have to be added back to make it ac-ceptable for drinking.

Technology is now available that can strip all the pollution from water and make it pure H_2O. However, water that has been purified by distillation and reverse osmosis is not pleasant to drink. While the best water to drink should be free of any smell, it is not taste-less. Good tasting water has a recipe of chemical ions and al-kalinity: cations and anions, minerals and salts.[5] These

> While the best water to drink should be free of any smell, it is not tasteless. Good tasting water has a recipe of chemical ions and alkalinity: cations and anions, minerals and salts.

Ice absorbs odors. It prevents water from releasing its volatile smells. It chills water to minimize its flavor. And much of the life on earth survives because when ice forms in water, it floats rather than sinks.

come to it naturally. Rain water percolates through the earth and picks up the local chemistry, developing *terrior*—its particular earth-based characteristics.

In the 18th and 19th centuries, in Europe especially but also in the US, people who could afford to take luxurious vacations went to spas and springs to bathe in and consume health-giving waters.[6] This was so popular that a business grew up to supply city folk with the natural, healthy, and wholesome spring waters from the country. The mineral water spas can have a hint of sulfur to them and the sulfur water is thought to provide health benefits.

However, a sulfur odor can be a mark of stagnant water, or swampy, decaying stench. The marshes and cesspools of the 18th and 19th centuries were considered unhealthy simply because of their smell which was thought to make people more vulnerable to diseases and death. Cedar swamp water was considered good and healthy when it was fresh and peaty.[3] It was when the water became stagnant that all the problems erupted, such as the emission of "mal-aria" or *bad air*. Black colored swamp water killed its fish and released strong odors that were considered miasmas or poisonous vapors. As a result of the low value placed on marshes and swampland, many cities filled them in to produce waterfronts of bustling industry. Today, we call these swamps *wetlands* and we place a high value on them for their purifying effects within a watershed, and because of their diverse ecology. But I'm not aware that they smell any different than the marshes and swamplands of old.

When I turned on the spigot to a bath tub in a hotel in Florida, the room filled with the smell of burnt match. The smoke alarm did not go off. The burnt match smell was due to the concentration of sulfur in the water, which was released when it was heated. I took my sulfur shower, but I did not see any improvements to my health as claimed by sulfur spring spas.

Flowing water purifies itself given time, dilution, exposure to sunlight, and the influx of oxygen. Running water, it was thought, had an unlimited capacity to cleanse itself of whatever was dumped into it. There's an Arab proverb that says, *When water turns over seven times it is purified.*[7] At first, microorganisms grow using the nutrients and food from the pollution that is dumped into the water. As they grow, they eat up the pollution. When the microorganisms eat up all their food, and on exposure to the sunlight, they die off, leaving the water in its more natural state. Unfortunately, with this naïve perspective, the waters of the world were polluted to the point of their death. The microorganisms that grow in the absence of oxygen, when waters are heavily loaded with pollution, are the most problematic. They create the bad stinks and contribute to fish mortality.

> Running water, it was thought, had an unlimited capacity to cleanse itself of whatever was dumped into it.

But not all microorganisms that grow in water produce such bad odors. Trichloroanisole creates an earthy, moldy smell in wine from bad corks. Trichloroanisole can also be produced by microorganisms that grow in water. The mold takes up chlorophenol from water and converts it to the more smelly chloroanisole. This is not good for drinking water but others have turned this around for our benefit. Knowing what smells are produced by microorganisms, we can grow them to make the odors we want.[8] Flavors and fragrances are produced by microorganisms more easily than by harvesting natural plants' stems, leaves, seeds, and fruit or even by chemical synthesis. The ability today to bio-engineer microorganisms that can make large quantities of desirable smelly molecules is a growing business. However, pleasant and desirable chemicals in one context can be quite problematic in another context. Compost is good when it smells musty and we apply it to the garden. A handful of dirt for the farmer can smell rich and fertile. But earthy or musty smelling water coming from the kitchen tap is not favorable at all, and can cost thousands of dollars a day in water treatment to control it so people won't complain.

I once smelled a stream that had no smell. We were taking samples from tributaries on the upper Schuylkill River to understand how the river changed in smell as it flowed downstream through farmland, towns, and into the city. This particular odorless stream flowed down from a coal mining region of the Blue Ridge. The pH was so low from acid mine drainage that nothing much lived in the stream. The water was very clear. It had no smell of vegetation. It had no smell at all.

Remember the water cycle we learned about in elementary school? Today we can explain the taste and smell of the water cycle. Good quality rain that deposits on the mountains picks up minerals from the local geology, producing a water recipe that is spring-water good assuming that the geology is favorable for good tasting water. Then it flows downstream through woodland, farmland, and suburban development where it gathers in lakes and behind dams, picking up the smell of decaying vegetation and algae. In rivers it picks up the fla-

Remember the water cycle we learned about in elementary school? Today we can explain the taste and smell of the water cycle.

vor of farm runoff, decaying organic matter, wastewater discharges, road runoff, and industrial activity. These smells are removed by drinking water treatment but then made stinky again as the used water travels back through sewers to the wastewater treatment plants, and back into the water cycle with its marshy-like aroma. Eventually it gets to the bay and the ocean where it tastes salty and smells like DMS. Is there a water cycle in the universe? Water is so important for life that we are looking for signs of water on other planets as an indication that extraterrestrial life exists. I wonder how we would describe the smell of water from Mars?

Over 97 percent of the water on Earth lies in the oceans and seas. Did you ever take salt water into your mouth? Ghastly stuff. Less than one percent of the earth's water is available for drinking, although we can make drinking water from ocean water. But the availability of fresh water is changing. We can see, smell, and taste the effects of climate change. Droughts produce water that tastes more salty due to the concentration of solids, or smells earthy due to the blooms of cyanobacteria. There will be less fresh water to dilute out all the wastewater we return to it, thus changing its smell. Floods will wash solids and pollution into the rivers. Wildfires will cause drastic and significant changes to water quality including its flavor, both immediately following the fire and years afterwards. With this in mind, we need to preserve all the fresh water we can so that we have something to pass on to future generations.

The average consumer expresses perceptions of water in very general terms such as *clear, cool,* and *clean.* While expert evaluators can pull apart flavor into its many components and are very discerning in this regard, that doesn't mean they can predict consumer perceptions. It's a different context. The average consumer uses snap decisions and first impressions to make everyday decisions.[9] And when untrained people are asked to slow down and think differently about their perceptions, they make different choices. Nonetheless, people use their senses to make decisions about the water they prefer to drink. And tap water has its distinct smells.

Here in the US we disinfect water with chlorine. We have been using chlorine now for more than 100 years, and it has saved many lives at a very reasonable cost. However, around 90 percent of public water systems are in towns and communities with less than 3,300 residents. For many years, because their drinking water came from wells, they didn't chlorinate it. They believed it was naturally purified. Today, they are being asked to chlorinate the water. Thus, in the US, public water should smell *chlorinous*. However, our customers prefer that their tap water not smell like chlorine, which is one of the reasons for bottled water being as popular as it is.

Maybe a squeeze of lemon juice can make the tap water better tasting. If you handle fish and want to remove the fishy smell, wash your hands with lemon juice. The lemon acidifies the fishy chemical so that, in its changed form, it will not volatilize and be smelled. But can lemon make water taste better? In upscale restaurants where a glass of water comes with a lemon wedge propped on the rim, the water is likely filtered or bottled—it has no chlorine in it. Take note, though, squirting lemon juice into tap water is something different because of the chlorine. Three drops of freshly squeezed lemon juice in an 8 ounce glass of tap water might be okay. You don't get the sour lemon juice flavor. The squirt of juice reduces the pH in water from 8 to 5, making it acidic, reducing the chlorine and its *chlorinous* flavor. But if the water contains chloramine, it changes the chemistry of the chloramine and brings out a swimming pool-like or *bleachy* smell. This might be a good smell for cleaning your bathroom, but not what you want in your tap water.

The battle between tap water and bottled water, and which tastes better, has been waged in the news. In one situation, a local TV station was on the lookout for a three minute, light-hearted story for prime time news following weather and sports. A consumer reporter was sent to cover our trained, expert tasters. He brought in bottled waters and asked us to tell him which one tasted the best. *But that's not what we do!* We demonstrated how a trained sensory team can dissect the flavors of bottled water, but we explained that each individual has to decide for himself what tastes best. As you may guess, news being what it is, the story ended up declaring that the cheaper bottled water was the best tasting.

> As scientists, we were annoyed. We wanted people to know we were using objective, scientific principles and careful data analysis to evaluate the flavor of water.

Another news reporter compared our trained panel to wine snobs, showing a dog pouncing about in the river to explain a *wet dog* odor. As scientists, we were annoyed. We wanted people to know we were using objective, scientific principles and careful data analysis to evaluate the flavor of water. We were using pre-screened glassware, a controlled testing temperature, a room with no odors or distractions, and people trained to smell and taste. Then the light bulb went off! We realized that the message we wanted to get out—that we personally taste the water our customers drink to make sure it's okay—actually was being told by the news.

Today, however, we don't wait for the evening news on TV, we get it in real time off the Internet. But the Internet provides accurate and inaccurate information without us always knowing which is which. Just Google the key words *water smells* and see what comes up: water smells like rotten eggs, onions, garlic, fish, gas, mold, metal, bleach, and just plain bad. And with information comes crowd opinion, which leads to information abuse and misuse, and misunderstanding. Handling news reporters was one thing, but now controlling what's on the Internet is something totally different!

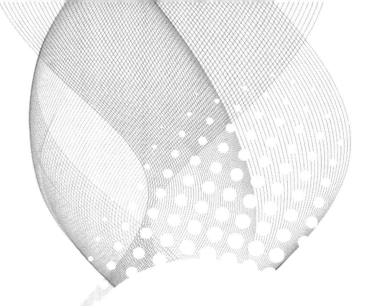

Less publicly, medical diagnosis in ancient Greece relied on taste to some extent. According to Galen, a patient's sweat should be tasted, the physician's tongue ascertaining its saltiness or acridity. Much could be learned: bitter tasting sweat hinted at jaundice, for example.

~ Mark M. Smith[1]

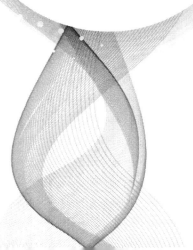

Chapter 8

Becoming a Part of History

At first I wanted to escape city life for the fields and forests, hugging trees and caring for flowers. This was what an ecologist was born to do. And throughout history, cities have been unhealthy places to live. Philadelphia was a struggling city between two polluted rivers. Its history meant nothing to me at the time. I only knew what I saw firsthand: industry, traffic, pollution.

Prior to the twentieth century, great cities like Paris and London were filled with the stench of too many people living too close together.[2] The streets were muddy and dotted with animal feces, splashed with whatever its residents threw out their windows and doors. Putrid odors arose from cesspools and cesspool cleaners, from slaughterhouses, breweries, wharves, and tanneries. People smelled according to their professions, from rope makers to candle makers, from butchers to dyers. The everyday person could not escape the smells of a hard life.

Philadelphia was no different. Hot and humid during the summer, Philadelphia's unpaved streets and lack of sewers made it an annoying city to live in. An 1875 *Report of the Water Supply for the City of Philadelphia* by its Commission of Engineers wrote: *The cobblestone streets were dirty and collected filth. Cesspools beneath the houses were overloaded.*

Flies were everywhere. Holes were dug to collect gutter water with all sorts of waste and dead animals. The river banks were swamps of washed up rotting debris. Stagnant water allowed mosquitoes to breed, which transferred Yellow Fever from person to person—a problem all along the eastern US coastline as ships brought infected people to port. Mosquitoes were thought to be a sign of the unwholesome atmosphere, not the actual cause of illness. Yellow Fever, or the Black Vomit, caused people to flee the city. But it was not from drinking water. It was a problem with stagnant water, with mosquitoes breeding in the stagnant water— mosquitoes that are lured to their victims by "smell."

Benjamin Rush, a signer of the Declaration of Independence, the first chair of chemistry in the US and a medical doctor, was intimately involved with Yellow Fever outbreaks during the late 1700s. While inspectors sniffed around muggy Philadelphia for causes, such as rotting coffee that had been left on a wharf, and decaying animal and vegetable matter, Dr. Rush applied blood-letting and purging with mercuric powder to cure his patients of illness. The French doctors used wine and tonic, and plenty of rest.[3] Let's not go back in time, but if we have to, I will choose the wine and rest option!

Outhouses, privies, and bathhouses were built over rivers and streams to move waste away. This seemed to make sense to the senses—out of sight and smell, out of mind. Then along came a better solution—to give each house its own cesspool or place to collect and concentrate the waste.[4] Out of the cesspools arose hazardous vapors and dangerous microbes from beneath the floor boards of overcrowded tenement houses.

As Philadelphia's population grew and houses became more crowded together, the cesspools seeped into the wells. The clear, cool, and good tasting well water was no longer safe. But the river water was turbid and had a vegetative, earthy smell. No one understood the concept of germs, that bacteria caused cholera, typhoid, and other diseases. So the residents preferred the cooler well water even though it was contaminated. In recalling the days of our Constitutional Convention, Catherine Drinker Bowen[5] wrote: *In summer, men had been seen to fall dead on the streets of Philadelphia after drinking cold water from the pumps [wells]. Bleeding was suggested, Moreau said, for those who drank too fast; some pumps bore a sign reading, "Death to him who drinks too quickly."*

Yellow Fever, and then cholera, and typhoid fever or "typhoid poison," motivated public health measures to try and put an end to the deaths. Cleaning streets, emptying cesspools, airing out hospitals, sniffing spices—many different attempts were tried. Then in 1799 the city formed a Watering Committee, which in 1888 gave the responsibility to find a solution to the Bureau of Water under the Department of Public Works.

Philadelphia did not choose to draw its water for public drinking from the Blue Ridge mountains. Instead the City chose to draw its water from the Delaware and Schuylkill rivers within sight of the city. Engineers and chemists tested the smell of the Schuylkill River from Philadelphia to the mountains, and found that it was not necessarily any better upriver. The Schuylkill River had, along its winding shoreline, many mills, breweries, bath houses, privies, farms, factories, and anthracite coal mines. So Philadelphia decided instead to protect the water within the city by establishing Fairmount Park along the banks of the Schuylkill River which was fresher, more turbulent, more aerated, and cooler than the Delaware River. The Delaware River had a decayed vegetation smell, although upstream in its headwaters it had a taste as good as spring water with only a trace of vegetable matter.

By the mid-1800s, the city had grown to half a million people. It was a leading textile and manufacturing center, and it needed a more reliable water supply. Water was pumped from the rivers with little or no treatment, through brick conduit, wooden tanks, and wooden or cast iron pipe.[6] The cast iron pipe affected the appearance and smell of the water, which was provided for free at public pumps around the city.

> The city's chemists smelled and tasted the water. An ideal drinking water was said to be clear, colorless, and sparkling as from a spring, refreshing in its coolness, and satisfying the aesthetic sense by its suggestion of purity.

The city's chemists smelled and tasted the water. An ideal drinking water was said to be clear, colorless, and sparkling as from a spring, refreshing in its coolness, and satisfying the aesthetic sense by its suggestion of purity.[7] Pumped Schuylkill water taken from hydrants and wooden mains, upon sitting for thirty-six hours, developed a marshy-decayed wood odor. The Schuylkill water also had an unpleasant earthy, peaty taste, or a vegetable-like smell. The chemists applied their laboratory tests to the problem; they defined water as either "normal" or "polluted" based on tests for ammonia, organic content, and oxygen demand.[8]

There was nothing anyone could do to improve the water that

was delivered through pipes in the city. The pollution of the rivers was uncontrolled and extensive. Hydrogen sulfide bubbled up from the organic sewage and mud. A list of pollution sources from the late 1800s includes: street gutters; household privies; street cleaners; factory privies and bath houses; naphtha waste from the gas company; lye from soap works; waste from hat factories and paper mills; dyes from wool mills; lime and salt and alum from tanneries; manure pile runoff; runoff from stables; waste oil from rolling mills; trash; iron and steel and coal wastes; and, railroad waste. In 1885, a water engineer wrote about a particular discharge: *The character of this discharge was very foul, sour to the taste and smelling strongly of spoiled beer.* Note that he actually tasted the water!

With the Industrial Revolution and the development following the end of the Civil War, the Schuylkill River in Philadelphia had become a stinking discharge.[9] Sewage floated down the river and bubbled from gases that were released from the black mud with the odor of putrefaction. The obnoxious odors were believed to be affecting everyone's health[10] and were signs of unsanitary conditions, unhealthy atmospheres, and a reduced personal resistance leading to susceptibility to disease.

When typhoid or cholera threatened Philadelphia, the citizens were advised to boil their tap water.[6] Encouraged by Louis Pasteur's research on fermentation and putrefaction, and Robert Koch's view through the microscope, the unseen world of microbes had come into view and the Golden Age of Bacteriology was launched, which led to the germ theory of disease. Water was a carrier of disease germs.[10]

Yet even with this new knowledge, into the 20th century, Philadelphians would fill water jugs for drinking from local springs that were not safe. Some of the springs ran too close to brick-lined sewers that inhaled and exhaled into the underground—pulling in groundwater and pushing out sewer water through the leaky brickwork. The Department of Public Health collected more than 1,800 samples from seventy-five springs. Not one was found to be free of fecal indicator bacteria or contamination! The city had to plug up the springs to stop people from filling their water jugs with unsafe water. Philadelphia needed a public water supply that the citizens could trust.

A hard battle to gain public acceptance was fought by sanitary engineers, bacteriologists, medical doctors, chemists, and public health officials. In the first decade of the 1900s, Philadelphia built drinking water treatment plants using sedimentation to get out the mud and filtration to remove the macroscopic contaminants. After Jersey City started chlorination in 1908, the boom in chlorination began.[11] Typhoid disease rates declined quite noticeably, so water treatment was hailed as a successful public health measure. But chlorinated water developed its own history of issues that continues to influence public perception and acceptance. People objected to the use of chlorine to disinfect their drinking water. It was thought to be a chemical poison.

The Schuylkill and Delaware rivers faced very challenging times during the first half of the 20th century. The Schuylkill River was toxic from coal mining residue and other wastes. The Delaware River essentially provided the city's secondary wastewater treatment, and it smelled like it. Although in 1914 the City developed its first master plan for sewers and sewage treatment, its three wastewater treatment plants were not put into service until the 1950s. Industries dumped their wastes into the rivers, intentionally as well as accidentally. Philadelphia's newspapers regularly took shots at the water supply especially since aircraft pilots could smell the river as they came into landing at the airport.

The smell of a now industrialized watershed was described as

Philadelphia's rich history includes good news and bad news about its water. While its rivers were once deadly to fish and obnoxious to smell, its water works were an engineering marvel.

oily, coal tar-like, aromatic, and *phenolic.* And these odors could be smelled in the drinking water even after chlorination. Locals called it a *chlorine cocktail.* A chemist, whose family moved to Philadelphia from a coal mine town in Pennsylvania to find work, recalled how his dad compensated for the tap water's flavor. He bought different soda pops —black cherry, orange, grape— and experimented with adding small amounts to a pitcher of tap water until the water was acceptable to drink.

> He bought different soda pops—black cherry, orange, grape—and experimented with adding small amounts to a pitcher of tap water until the water was acceptable to drink.

As the rivers cleaned up, they did not necessarily get better. Once toxic rivers became nutrient rich rivers, algae—the stinky kind—started taking up residence. When water goes through redemption it can become quite troublesome. Muddy water inhibits algae growth because it prevents light from penetrating into the water. Algae need the light for photosynthesis, their daytime metabolic energy engine. Once water clears up, algae find a new frontier for growth. This happened in the Great Lakes. Blooms of algae and cyanobacteria that are toxic and odorous find the clearer, nutrient-rich waters great places to grow.

My city had grown from about 600 people in 1683 to 12,000 people in 1731, to over 1 million people in 1900, and over 2 million people in 1950. In 1951, Philadelphia formed the Philadelphia Water Department under a Home Rule City Charter. The Water Department was now able to pursue capital improvements that would finally change the water situation.

As sewage, industrial discharges, and spills came under control in the 1960s, the rivers started to shed their hydrogen sulfide, marshy, sewage, hydrocarbon, and phenolic stinks. The dissolved oxygen level in the Delaware River, or estuary, as it flowed past Philadelphia contained less than 2 ppm during the summer. Most fish prefer 5 ppm or more. With wastewater no longer being discharged directly to the rivers, the oxygen level increased such that today the river supports a healthy diversity of fish.

The drinking water paralleled this change but kept its earthy-musty flavor in addition to the varying chlorine smell as the art of chlorination advanced, and breakpoint chlorination produced a more stable and safer finished product. The Philadelphia Water Department's annual report from its Water Treatment Section, in 1966, stated the following: *The water quality other than the sensory aspect is excellent, but the customer very rarely complains about a little turbidity in his water. Usually, 90% of the time he complains about the palatability. Therefore, I recommend that for 1967 we make a strong attempt to upgrade the sensory quality of the water by eliminating the musty taste and odor.*

A musty taste—that's all? This was good news!

I was born in the 1950s when the city started losing its population to the suburbs. Mills, manufacturing centers, and factories had shut down. The city lost about a half million people. And those who moved to the suburbs did not want anything Philadelphia-like following them. However, the city they left behind began building better sewers and modern wastewater treatment plants. The drinking water system took a turn for the better, perhaps for the second time in the city's history. One of the nation's most modern water treatment plants was built, showcasing the new age of treatment technology. Plans were put in motion to develop a modernized control system for the distribution network. Capital projects were at an all-time high. The city was on the rebound.

This is the situation that I stepped into when I decided to make water the subject of my career. But it would take another twenty-five years to turn this safer water into better tasting water. Even with an advanced laboratory of professional chemists, biologists, and engineers, and the analytical ability to detect contaminants down to a nanogram per liter, we still needed the human nose to guide us to improve the water's flavor.[12,13] Water and the human senses have always been intertwined. This connection became part of my story and it influenced Philadelphia's history.

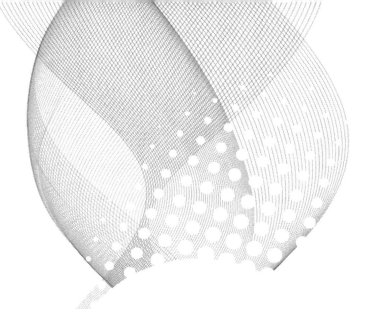

Fragrance has the instantaneous and invisible power to penetrate consciousness with pure pleasure. Scent reaches us in ways that elude sight and sound but conjure imagination in all its sensuality, unsealing hidden worlds.

~ Mandy Aftel[1]

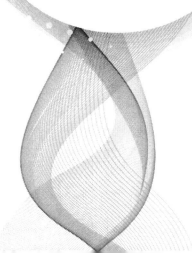

Chapter 9
Imagine the Possibilities

Throughout history, people have lived in colorful smellscapes.[2] Scents have purified, protected, preserved, made offerings acceptable to the gods, and even changed the bad to good. If you could afford it, you scented everything around you and on you—your body, your clothes, and even your pets. Every room in your house and every floor, fireplace, storeroom, bedroom, and kitchen was scented. Religious ceremonies, parades, and funerals were scented. Food, wine, and water were scented.

If you were not rich enough to control your smellscape, then the smells of life defined you—you took on the odors of your occupation, the animals you brought into your home at night, and the food you ate. These natural scents—onion, garlic, herbs, burnt wood, decaying matter, human and animal waste—defined your place in your community.

Treatments were developed for counteracting malodors such as by soaking things in vinegar. If that didn't work, you could consider burning aromatics, sprinkling with perfume, making sachets of flowers, spreading herbs and garlic, carrying amulets, soaking sponges in camphor, or even burning gunpowder. If you could overcome a bad smell with a good smell then you could protect your health. If you couldn't neutralize human and animal waste by removing their stench[3] then you could change their smell using orange, lemon, cloves, or other aromatic substances as well as lilac, lime, and pine.

Today we have gone to the extreme of bringing some smells to the edge of extinction. The breeding of roses to produce hardy, colorful flowers that can be shipped around the world has resulted in the gradual loss of the well-known fragrance of the rose.[4] So what do we do? We fake the rose smell using scents such as 2-phenylethanol. But it's a poor copy of a rose. The natural smell consists of a well-designed composition of fragrant chemicals that act like musical notes played by an orchestra. Listen to the tuba or the French horn by itself, and you won't hear the masterpiece that was created for the full orchestra.

> These fragrant chemicals affect us emotionally, physically, sexually, and socially. They are one way we know ourselves and each other.

These fragrant chemicals affect us emotionally, physically, sexually, and socially. They are one way we know ourselves and each other.[5] But fragrances can also make people feel sick. Halifax, Nova Scotia passed a law against wearing perfume and cologne in public because some people may be overly sensitive, although it has yet to be proven that people can be genetically disposed to feeling sick after smelling fragrances.[6]

Today we have cleaners, deodorizers, and scented candles to infuse our smellscape with chosen scents. We purchase an array of deodorants, perfumes, colognes, massage oils, lotions, soaps, hand creams, shampoos, and body sprays. Devices puff out odors from computers, alarm clocks, and phones. Little scented puffers plug into the wall outlet and diffuse different scents at different times of the day. Taken to a larger scale, environmental fragrancing controls the odorous atmosphere of department stores, hotels, factories, and offices so as to influence our mood and mental state. Scents make factory workers more efficient, relax people in their hotel rooms, sustain shoppers in department stores, brand products, improve test takers' scores, help soldiers work through post-traumatic stress, increase gambling in casinos, provide an enhanced massage treatment, and reduce stress in medical patients.

Really bad smells, though, can make us feel sick. That is why detectives and coroners use tricks to minimize the smell of death. They smoke cigars or rub Vaseline under their noses, or use products such as OdorScreen[7] which contains a mix of chemicals in Vaseline that can be applied above the upper lip to minimize the inhalation of sickening odors.

Despite all of this investment into controlling our smellscape, Aristotle claimed that smelling was for the animals. René Descartes said that the sense of smell was the inferior of all senses. In 18th century Europe, the beautiful were not supposed to have a scent. Then, in the 19th century, the role of scent became romanticized, evoking emotion and memory, and even providing insights into life and death. Writers and poets pondered the spiritual role of scent. French poet Charles Baudelaire claimed that there is no bad smell, whereas Immanuel Kant dreamed of losing his sense of smell, and Sigmund Freud taught that civilized man does not need his sense of smell; that a fascination with smell was unhealthy.

> Eating is an emotional experience because it is a multi-sensory experience based on taste, smell, sight, sound, pain, touch, and temperature.

I wonder how many of these great minds enjoyed the sensory pleasures of eating and drinking? Eating is an emotional experience because it is a multi-sensory experience based on taste, smell, sight, sound, pain, touch, and temperature. And foods affect our emotions by causing the release of endorphins and serotonin.[8]

Since smell is integral to our enjoyment of food, we are changing the way we create and serve food. Food pairing, or the art of matching appetizers, entrées, drinks, and deserts is now a science linked to the chemistry of flavor. With the help of analytical chemistry, we can pull apart the components that make up the flavor of food and beverages so that we can piece them back together in complementary ways to pair foods and beverages for greater culinary creativity and enjoyment.

Over 800 chemicals are in coffee, but less than thirty make up its desired flavor.[9] Over 250 chemicals are in a strawberry, but only about five make up its trademark flavor.[10] And if you smell these five chemicals one at a time, you would not smell a strawberry but rather cotton candy, creamy peach, guava, pineapple, and cut grass. While more than 600 chemicals can be detected in chocolate, only about twenty-five make up the key ingredients that give it a distinguishable flavor.[11] But if you taste these chemicals one at a time, you might even be disgusted with some of the smells that come from the individual components of fine chocolate.

The better we understand how we experience food, the more creative we can be in altering that experience. Take a sip of coffee from a spoon instead of straight from the cup, or lift a slice of strawberry to your mouth on a spoon instead of using your fingers, and you change the sensory experience. Spoons made of different materials alter the sensory experience.[12] Spoons made of copper, iron, and zinc impart a metallic retronasal flavor and a bitter taste. If you like to suck on a spoon, you might not enjoy this unless you serve ice cream on it, in which case the flavor might be enhanced. Gold and chrome spoons appear to impart no taste, whereas silver spoons can be bitter. Hopefully you were not born with a silver spoon in your mouth!

But if the fork or spoon concerns you, you can scent it so that when you raise the food to your mouth, your nose smells the scent borne by the utensil. The size, shape, and makeup of the spoon can be changed to help us eat differently, to enhance flavor, and even to make the experience fun. Spoon technology can help dieters achieve their goals, train children to eat healthier food, and monitor food intake.

Not only does the material makeup of the cup or spoon influence our sensory experience, but its round, square, or angular shape affects our experience.[13] Rounded shapes denote sweet foods whereas angular shapes suggest bitter foods, or carbonated beverages. Thus, spicy foods should be served on triangular plates.

Regular water, then, would be served in something round. We already have round drinking glasses, round spigots, and round pipes. Yet a mineral water that is carbonated should be served in an angular glass. Are we tricking the brain to change its perceptions or just giving our brain what it wants? And the color of the glass also affects our sensory experience—perhaps just in our brains where the sensory inputs play on each other.

Our ambient environment affects how we experience food. We can change the dining experience by changing sound, color, lighting, and temperature. When I was growing up, families gathered around the TV and ate prepackaged TV dinners together, laughing

Water touches on all our senses. Clear, cool, and refreshing, we enjoy the soothing sound of the babbling creek or the washing of the waves on the beach. And we relax with its warm caress of our bodies.

at the quaint, family-friendly comedy shows. Perhaps the entertainment made the just-heat-to-eat food taste better.

A relaxing or romantic feeling can be generated by turning down the lights, turning on some jazz music, and lighting a candle. How about changing the experience of sight, sound, and smell to resemble the seashore when you eat lobster, or to remind you of a mountain

> Our ambient environment affects how we experience food. We can change the dining experience by changing sound, color, lighting, and temperature.

chateau when you dine on rainbow trout? Or maybe you want to be in Paris or Rome or Seoul. Digital menus can help us do all of this—guiding our food pairing, making music selections, and changing our visual surroundings. The placemat, plates, and table can change color and temperature based on what food you order to enhance your dining experience.

Maybe all of this technology to control our smellscape and to mimic our senses will be used to enhance our homes. Imagine, after a long day at work, your home recognizes you by your eyes and fingerprints, and prepares for your entry. Room temperature warms or cools based on the season of the year. Your pre-selected music, and complimentary lighting, set the mood. Food starts cooking. Drinks are poured. Bath water is prepared. Then your entertainment pod prepares an after-dinner show—an ultimate theatre experience using multi-sensory forms of entertainment.

I'm not one for the exercise gym; running on a treadmill, watching a small TV half a room away, listening to music from a headset while smelling warm rubber and human sweat. But what if I could step into an exercise pod at home and choose a walk around a lake with the smell of pine trees, the sound of birds, and wind through the trees? This I would do. Add to that the feel of sand on bare feet, like running on the beach. Imagine what exercising could be like!

Now if you have a dog then take it for walks to get some exercise, and loosen the leash to let your dog sniff whatever it wants to sniff. A dog has ten to forty times more receptors in its nose than you do.[9] Trained dogs sniff for drugs, dead people in rubble, bombs, and animal scat. Dogs can also sniff human skin for diseases, detect colorectal cancer, and smell lung cancer on our breath. Dogs can indeed be man's best friend, or perhaps man's best nose!

If you are not the type to own a dog that checks your health, you can walk through a sensory detector that sniffs you using an electronic nose. Sensory proteins from the noses of mice placed on nano-materials have been used to make chemical sensors.[14] An e-nose can now do what servants to the king did a long time ago— smell pee and poop for signs of illness. Since medical doctors no longer take the time to smell our breath or pinch our skin, perhaps we need something to fill the gap!

Right alongside the e-nose is the e-tongue. Since the sense of taste is based on the flow of electrons as induced by chemicals, taste can be measured electronically with electronic tongues. If cooking is something you like to do to relax at home, you can perhaps be a master chef. What if the e-tongue could test food to determine whether it has just the right level of spice as directed by an online cookbook? You could make gourmet meals as if the chef were standing over you, watching and dipping her finger in the sauce to approve or disapprove according to her personal taste. Imagine how this could improve everyday life! Not only would cooking be a form of relaxation, but better tasting food would be a comfort, especially when it is paired with a complementary bottle of wine.

Finally, all of these advancements and technologies can be applied to water for the testing of its safety, its recipe for enjoyment, and its use for bathing, swimming, relaxation, and therapy. Imagine waking up and beside your bed is a cup of fresh water chilled to 10°F below room temperature to help your body rehydrate after a night's sleep. You jump in the shower, which is already warmed and scented with a fresh, invigorating fragrance. As you leave for work, you strap onto your wrist your digital, personal health tracker that guides your level of hydration through the day. This is important since hydration affects your appearance, digestion, blood flow, brain activity, physical movement, mood, and excretion of toxins. Imagine all these possibilities!

The taste of water influences what we prefer to drink: mineral water, sparkling water, spring water, or tap water—even flavored water. Different waters are selected to pair with different foods. And sports water is fortified with vitamins and electrolytes. Once water from springs and spas could be bottled and distributed, the belief in the medicinal, health-giving properties of water made its way into our homes.[15] Perhaps we can have a home dispenser that provides health-giving water or mineral water according to our needs and desires.

When it comes to smell, water should have no smell when we drink it. It should be refreshing with no aftertaste. But water applied to a garden might induce a fresh mulch smell. Bath water could be scented. And how about including scents into fountains. We already have light shows at fountains. The sense of smell has been used with art, so why not with fountains? Maybe, in the art museum, a painting of the sea could smell like the sea, and a painting of a woodland stream could smell like pine, hemlock, and laurel. Why not?

Consider also the appearance of water: clear water for a mountain stream or a glass of water from the tap; or deep blue and green for the tropical islands. Why not choose the color of water you want? When bathing, I want aqua-blue, tropical colored water. When drinking, crystal clear. When watering my lawn, I think my neighbors would prefer green.

The sound of water is important: the sound of water from rain or a shower; of steam from a tea pot; of a babbling brook; or of waves on the beach. So why not infuse your home with the sound of water? We know that the taste of food or its enjoyment is affected by the things we hear while we eat.[16] Carbonated beverages provide the sound of tiny bubbles popping, i.e. the fizz. Sour tastes match higher pitch sounds, whereas bitter tastes match lower pitch sounds. Wine matched to certain music tastes better than wine consumed in silence. And different wines can be matched to different musical pieces for greater enjoyment. So why not use the sound of water to help us relax, or energize, or exercise?

Sometimes we are limited in possibilities by what we have been taught. We have been educated by early schooling to think in terms of only five senses: smell, sight, taste, vision, hearing, and touch. However, we should appreciate all *nine* senses. We also have senses for pain, temperature, balance, and movement (or the kinesthetic sense). Eating and drinking clearly involve the senses of taste and smell. Mouth feel, or touch, is important, too, such as in detecting the freshness of food. The way our food looks affects our sensory experience, too. Isn't that why gourmet chefs decorate their plates so artfully?

So add to the five sensory experiences the temperature of our food and the spiciness that involves pain sensations. While the sense of balance may not apply to eating and drinking, the movement of our jaw and related joints does influence the eating experience. So, it seems that eight of our nine senses are involved when we dine.

Why not also when we come in contact with water?

What about the other senses? Water clearly plays a role in pain management, and in controlling temperature. Exercising in water can help us with balance and with our kinesthetic disorders.

Water touches on all nine senses in profound ways such that the sensory experience of water can be powerfully enhanced in everyday life, in art, in healthcare, in entertainment, and in our communities.

Water touches on all nine senses in profound ways such that the sensory experience of water can be powerfully enhanced in everyday life, in art, in healthcare, in entertainment, and in our communities.

Imagine the possibilities we have today to enrich our lives based on our knowledge of the human senses. And then add to that the increasing awareness in the world of the value of water, and how the sensory experience of water connects with that vital life force. It's exciting!

And it's all a part of my career. That's exciting to me! I can understand how I came to have a career in water—so much of my life has been touched by water from fishing, to swimming, to canoeing, to watering the lawn, and watching a rain storm come and go. But how I came to know so much about the human senses is a surprise. I could never have predicted that journey.

I was the first undergraduate to enroll in the Environmental Science program at my university. I thought I would be a naturalist, protecting our fields, woodlands, and streams. I was headed toward becoming a botanist when I met a professor who introduced me to water. I realized I could become a water scientist. And it seemed a worthwhile career to invest in.

I always liked the idea of being a scientist. There's something special about the title. It's associated with discovery, exploration, and knowledge—of solving puzzles and finding solutions. That's what I stepped into when I began studying the way things taste and smell. When it came to solving problems about the flavor of water and the smell of wastewater, I accepted the challenge and soaked up the science of the human senses. As a result, I came to appreciate my own senses in everyday life. I networked and learned from experts, and then I taught others what I learned.

Not many scientists have been granted the time and resources to study the flavor of water in all its various uses and forms. This unique experience enhanced my life and opened doors to travel the world, make lifetime friends, and contribute to the advancement of the science of water, while becoming a part of its history. Through my career in water and my studies of the human senses, I was able to connect with co-workers, researchers, and scientists— with water professionals regionally, nationally, and even globally, and with news reporters, students, customers, and neighbors.

Such a worthwhile career gives purpose to life, and it comes about through the investments we make in the opportunities we embrace and the people we work with. Some of these opportunities come unexpectedly; I believe providentially. All in all, the fact remains that when we embrace them, and see them for the treasures they are, we enrich our lives beyond measure. Imagine the possibilities!

NOTES

Chapter 1 – Going with the Flow

[1] T. Standage. 2005. *A History of the World in 6 Glasses*. Walker & Company, New York, New York. p.273.

[2] A.M. Pederson, A. Bardow, S.B. Jensen, and B. Nauntofte. 2002. Saliva and gastrointestinal functions of taste, mastication, swallowing and digestion. *Oral Diseases* 8:117-129.

[3] J.M. Brunstrom, A.W. Macrae and B. Roberts. 1997. Mouth-state dependent changes in the judged pleasantness of water at different temperatures. *Physiology and Behavior* 61(5) 667-669.

[4] W.P. Mason. 1896. *Water-Supply: Considered Principally from a Sanitary Standpoint*. John Wiley & Sons, New York, New York.

[5] American Water Works Association. 2006. Are You Drinking Enough Water? www.awwa.org accessed on December 10, 2006.

[6] H. Valtin. 2002. Drink at least eight glasses of water a day. Really? Is there scientific evidence for "8x8"? *American Journal of Physiology – Regulatory, Integrative and Comparative Physiology* 282:R993-R1004.

[7] D. Negoianu and S. Goldfarb. 2008. Just add water. *Journal of the American Society of Nephrology* 19:1-2.

[8] A.G. Ershow and K.P. Cantor. 1989. *Total Water and Tapwater Intake in the United States: Population-based Estimates of Quantities and Sources*. National Cancer Institute, Bethesda, Maryland.

[9] Food and Nutrition Board, Institute of Medicine, National Academy of Sciences Panel of Dietary Reference Intakes for Electrolytes and Water. 2004. *Dietary Reference Intakes (DRI) for Water*. The National Academies Press, Washington, D.C.

[10] T. Standage. 2005. *A History of the World in 6 Glasses*. Walker & Company, New York, New York.

[11] M. Mascha. 2006. *Fine Waters*. Quirk Books, Philadelphia, Pennsylvania.

[12] L. Huerta-Saenz, M. Irigoyen, J. Benavides and M. Mendoza. 2012. Tap or bottled water: drinking preferences among urban minority children and adolescents. *Journal of Community Health* 37:54-58.

[13] H. Marcussen, P.E. Holm and H.C.C. Hansen. 2013. Composition, flavor, chemical foodsafety, and consumer preferences of bottled water. *Comprehensive Reviews in Food Science and Food Safety* 12:333-352.

[14] S. Maxwell. 2012. Water is still cheap: demonstrating the true value of water. *Journal of the American Water Works Association* 104(5) 31-37.

[15] See www.un.org/waterforlifedecade, accessed on October 20, 2014.

Chapter 2 – Learning to Smell

[1] R. Herz. 2007. *The Scent of Desire*. Harper Perrenial, New York, New York. pp. 237-238.

[2] P. Breckenridge. 2009. Bunnies twitch their noses for information. *The San Francisco Chronicle*, October 7, page E-7.

[3] A. Gilbert. 2008. *What the Nose Knows: The Science of Scent in Everyday Life*. Crown Publishers, New York, New York.

[4] D. Ackerman. 1990. *A Natural History of the Senses*. Vintage Books, New York, New York.

[5] R. Herz. 2007. *The Scent of Desire*. HarperCollins Publishers, New York, New York.

[6] C. Bushdid, M.O. Magnasco, L.B. Vosshall, and A. Keller. 2014. Humans can discriminate more than 1 trillion olfactory stimuli. *Science* 343: 1370-1372.

[7] C. Classen, D. Howes, and A. Synnott. 1994. *Aroma – The Cultural History of Smell*. Routledge, New York, New York.

[8] H.T. Lawless and H. Heymann. 1998. *Sensory Evaluation of Food: Principles and Practices*. International Thomson Publishing, New York, New York.

[9] R.S. Smith, R.L. Doty, G.A. Burlingame, and D.A. McKeown. 1993. Smell and taste function in the visually impaired. *Perception and Psychophysics* 54(5) 649-655.

Chapter 3 – Playing the Detective

[1] M. Birnbaum. 2011. *Season to Taste*. HarperCollins Publishers, New York, New York. p. 122.

[2] M. Petracco. 2005. Our everyday cup of coffee: the chemistry behind its magic. *Journal of Chemical Education* 82(8) 1161-1166.

[3] J.L. Graham, K.A. Loftin, M.T. Meyer, and A.C. Ziegler. 2010. Cyanotoxin mixtures and taste-and-odor compounds in cyanobacterial blooms from the Midwestern United States. *Environmental Science and Technology* 44(19) 7361-7368.

[4] J. Raloff. 2007. Aquatic non-scents. *Science News* 171(4) 59-60.

[5] P. Omur-Ozbek and A. M. Dietrich. 2011. Retronasal perception and flavor thresholds of iron and copper in drinking water. *Journal of Water and Health* 9(1) 1-9.

[6] S. Mirlohi, A.M. Dietrich, and S. E. Duncan. 2011. Age-associated variation in sensory perception of iron in drinking water and the potential for overexposure in the human population. *Environmental Science and Technology* 45(15) 6575-6583.

Chapter 4 – Making Connections

[1] A. Corbin. 1986. *The Foul and the Fragrant – Odor and the French Social Imagination*. Harvard University Press, Cambridge, Massachusetts. p. 15.

[2] J. Palmer and C. Kaminski. 2013. *Water: A Comprehensive Guide for Brewers*. Brewers Publications, Boulder, Colorado.

[3] A. Corbin. 1986. *The Foul and the Fragrant – Odor and the French Social Imagination*. Harvard University Press, Cambridge, Massachusetts.

[4] J.C. Thresh and J.F. Beale. 1925. *The Examination of Water and Water Supplies* (3rd ed). P. Blakiston's Son & Co., Philadelphia, Pennsylvania.

[5] E.B. Phelps. 1944. *Stream Sanitation*. John Wiley & Sons, Inc., New York, New York.

[6] G.C. Whipple, G.M. Fair and M.C. Whipple. 1948. *The Microscopy of Drinking Water*, (4th ed). John Wiley and Sons, Inc., New York, New York.

[7] ITV. 2013. Cut grass smell is "key to healthier dairy products". www.itv.com/news/wales/update/2013-08-22/cut-grass-smell-is-key-to-healthier-dairy-products accessed on August 22, 2013.

[8] American Public Health Association. 1946. *Standard Methods for the Examination of Water and Sewage* (9th ed). Boyd Printing Co., Inc., Albany, New York.

[9] G.M. Fair and W. F. Wells. 1934. The air-dilution method of odor determination in water analysis. *Journal of the American Water Works Association* 26:1670-1683.

[10] J.K. Lazo, J.L. Pratt, C.N. Herrick, M.L. Hagestand, R.S. Raucher, R.E. Hurd, and E.H. Rambo. 2004. Understanding and enhancing the impact of consumer confidence reports. In: *Efficient and Customer-Responsive Organization*. Water Research Foundation, Denver, Colorado.

[11] E.D. Mackey, J. Davis, L. Boulos, J.C. Brown, and G.F. Crozes. 2003. *Customer Perceptions of Tap Water, Bottled Water, and Filtration Devices.* Water Research Foundation, Denver, Colorado.

[12] E.D. Mackey, H. Baribeau, A.C. Fonseca, J. Davis, L. Boulos, J.C. Brown, G.F. Crozes, P. Piriou, J.M. Rodrigues, M. Fouret, A. Bruchet, and D.J. Hiltebrand. 2004. *Public Perception of Tap Water Chlorinous Flavor.* Water Research Foundation, Denver, Colorado.

[13] M. De F. Doria, N. Pidgeon, and P.R. Hunter. 2009. Perceptions of drinking water quality and risk and its effect on behavior: a cross-national study. *The Science of the Total Environment* 407(21) 271-276.

[14] M.J. McGuire. 1995. Off-flavour as the consumer's measure of drinking water safety. *Water Science and Technology* 31(11) 1-8.

[15] A.M. Dietrich and G.A. Burlingame. 2015. Critical review and rethinking of USEPA secondary standards for maintaining organoleptic quality of drinking water. *Environmental Science & Technology* 49(2) 708-720.

[16] H.R. Moskowitz. 1993. Sensory analysis procedures and viewpoints: intellectual history, current debates, future outlooks. *Journal of Sensory Studies* 8:241-256.

[17] R. Desrochers. 2008. Sensory analysis in the water industry. *Journal of the American Water Works Association* 100(10) 50-54.

Chapter 5 – Taking a Detour

[1] A. Gilbert. 2008. *What the Nose Knows – The Science of Scent in Everyday Life.* Crown Publishers, New York, New York. p. 81.

[2] D. Laporte. 2000. *History of Shit.* MIT Press, Cambridge, Massachusetts.

[3] J. Erdmann. 2008. Rotten remedy. *Science News* 173(10) 152-153.

[4] R.G. Buttery, D.G. Guadagni, L.C. Ling, R.M. Seifert, and W. Lipton. 1976. Additional volatile components of cabbage, broccoli, and cauliflower. *Journal of Agricultural and Food Chemistry* 24(4) 829-832.

[5] H. Kubota, A. Mitani, Y. Niwano, K. Takeuchi, A. Tanaka, N. Yamaguchi, Y. Kawamura, and J. Hitomi. 2012. Moraxella species are primarily responsible for generating malodor in laundry. *Applied and Environmental Microbiology* 78(9) 3317-3324.

[6] A. Gilbert. 2008. *What the Nose Knows*. Crown Publishers, New York.

[7] X. Cheng, M. Wodarczyk, R. Lendzinski, E. Peterkin, and G.A. Burlingame. 2009. Control of DMSO in wastewater to prevent DMS nuisance odors. *Water Research* 43:2989-2998.

[8] T. Holt. 2007. The science of yummy. *Popular Science* 271(5) 46-52.

[9] D. Ackerman. 1990. *A Natural History of the Senses*. Vintage Books, New York, New York.

[10] S. O'Connell. 2009. The science behind that fresh seaside smell. *The Telegraph* http://www.telegraph.co.uk/science/6044238/The-science-behind-that-fresh-seaside-smell.html accessed on September 4, 2009.

[11] R.L. Doty. 1995. Introduction and Historical Perspective. In: *Handbook of Olfaction and Gustation*. Mercel Dekker, Inc., New York, New York.

Chapter 6 – Telling Stories

[1] D. Ackerman. 1995. *A Natural History of the Senses*. Vintage Books, New York, New York. pp. 6-7.

[2] See www.flavornet.org.

[3] R.L. Doty. 2010. *The Great Pheromone Myth*. The Johns Hopkins University Press, Baltimore, Maryland.

[4] D. Ackerman. 1990. *A Natural History of the Senses*. Vintage Books, New York, New York.

[5] D. Khiari, L. Brenner, G.A. Burlingame, and I.H. Suffet. 1992. Sensory gas chromatography for evaluation of taste and odor events in drinking water. *Water Science and Technology* 25(2) 97-104.

[6] Japan Probe. 2007. Coming soon: Pepsi Ice Cucumber. *Japan Probe* http://www.japanprobe.com/2007/05/24/coming-soon-pepsi-ice-cucumber/ accessed on May 3, 2013.

[7] P. Schieberle, S. Ofner, and W. Grosch. 1990. Evaluation of potent odorants in cucumbers (*Cucumis sativus*) and muskmelons (*Cucumis melo*) by aroma extract dilution analysis. *Journal of Food Science* 55(1) 193-195.

8 J. Orgill, A. Shaheed, J. Brown, and M. Jeuland. 2013. Water quality perceptions and willingness to pay for clean water in peri-urban Cambodian communities. *Journal of Water and Health* 11(3) 489-506.

9 M.K. Goetz. 2013. The paradox of value: water rates and the law of diminishing marginal utility. *Journal of the American Water Works Association* 105(9)57-59.

Chapter 7 – Testing the Waters

1 B. Kingsolver. 2010. Water is Life. *National Geographic* 217(4) p. 44.

2 D. Tuhas. 2012. Storm scents: it's true, you can smell oncoming summer rain. *Scientific American.* www.scientificamerican.com/article.cfm?id= storm-scents-smell-rain&print=true accessed on July 25, 2012.

3 W.P. Mason. 1896. *Water-Supply: Considered Principally from a Sanitary Standpoint.* John Wiley & Sons, Inc., New York, New York.

4 A.R. Leeds. 1884. *Preliminary Report of a Chemical Investigation into the Present and Proposed Future Water Supply of Philadelphia.* Bureau of Water, Philadelphia, Pennsylvania.

5 G.A. Burlingame, A. M. Dietrich, and A. J. Whelton. 2007. Understanding the basics of tap water taste. *Journal of the American Water Works Association* 99(5) 100-111.

6 F.H. Chapelle. 2005. *Wellsprings – A Natural History of Bottled Spring Water.* Rutgers University Press, New Brunswick, New Jersey.

7 E.B. Phelps. 1944. *Stream Sanitation.* John Wiley & Sons, Inc., New York, New York.

8 M.M. Bomgardener. 2012. The sweet smell of microbes. *Chemical and Engineering News*, July 16, pp25-29. www.CEN-online.org accessed on May 14, 2013.

9 M. Gladwell. 2005. *Blink: The Power of Thinking Without Thinking.* Little, Brown and Company, New York, New York.

Chapter 8 – Becoming a Part of History

1 M. Smith. 2007. *Sensing the Past: Seeing, Hearing, Smelling, Tasting, and Touching in History.* University of California Press, Berkeley, California. p. 75.

[2] A. Corbin. 1986. *The Foul and the Fragrant – Odor and the French Social Imagination*. Harvard University Press, Cambridge, Massachusetts.

[3] J.H. Powell. 1993. *Bring Out Your Dead: The Great Plague of Yellow Fever in Philadelphia in 1793*. University of Pennsylvania Press, Philadelphia, Pennsylvania.

[4] D. Laporte. 2000. *History of Shit*. MIT Press, Cambridge, Massachusetts.

[5] C.D. Bowen. 1966. *Miracle at Philadelphia – The Story of the Constitutional Convention*. Atlantic Monthly Press Book, Little, Brown and Co., Boston, Massachusetts.

[6] M. P. McCarthy.1987. *Typhoid and the Politics of Public Health in Nineteenth-Century Philadelphia*. American Philosophical Society, Philadelphia, Pennsylvania.

[7] E.H. Richards. 1900. *Air, Water, and Food – from a Sanitary Standpoint*. John Wiley and Sons, New York, New York.

[8] W.P. Mason. 1896. *Water-Supply: Considered Principally from a Sanitation Standpoint*. John Wiley and Sons, New York, New York.

[9] J.F. Lewis. 1924. *The Redemption of the Lower Schuylkill*. Enterprise Publishing Co., Burlington, New Jersey.

[10] W.T. Sedgwick. 1914. *Principles of Sanitary Science and the Public Health: with Special Reference to the Causation and Prevention of Infectious Diseases*. The MacMillan Co., New York, New York.

[11] M.J. McGuire. 2013. *The Chlorine Revolution: Water Disinfection and the Fight to Save Lives*. American Water Works Association, Denver, Colorado.

[12] G.A. Burlingame. 2010. *Taste at the Tap: A Consumer's Guide to Tap Water Flavor*. American Water Works Association, Denver, Colorado.

[13] G.A. Burlingame, S.D.J. Booth, A. Bruchet, A. M. Dietrich, D. L. Gallagher, D. Khiari, I.H. (Mel) Suffet, and S. B. Watson. 2011. *Diagnosing Taste and Odor Problems Field Guide*. American Water Works Association, Denver, Colorado.

Chapter 9 – Imagine the Possibilities

[1] M. Aftel. 2001. *Essence and Alchemy – A Natural History of Perfume*. Gibbs Smith, Publishers, Salt Lake City, Utah. p.11.

[2] C. Classen, D. Howes and A. Synnott. 1994. *Aroma – The Cultural History of Smell*. Routledge, New York, New York.

[3] D. Laporte. 2000. *History of Shit*. MIT Press, Cambridge, Massachusetts.

[4] I. Amato. 2005. Save the flowers. *Science News*. 168(13) 202-204.

[5] R. Herz. 2007. *The Scent of Desire*. HarperCollins Publishers, New York, New York.

[6] C. Nickerson. 2000. Perfume ban raising a stink in Halifax, city forbids scented products in public. *The Boston Globe*, May 28.

[7] See www.odorscreenusa.com accessed on December 29, 2011.

[8] D. Ackerman. 1990. *A Natural History of the Senses*. Vintage Books, New York, New York.

[9] A. Gilbert. 2008. *What the Nose Knows: The Science of Scent in Everyday Life*. Crown Publishers, New York, New York.

[10] T. Holt. 2007. The science of yummy. *Popular Science* 271(5) 46-52.

[11] C. Arnold. 2011. The sweet smell of chocolate: sweat, cabbage and beef. *Scientific American* at http://www.scientificamerican.com/article.cfm?id=sensonics-chocolate-smell, accessed on November 4, 2011.

[12] Z. Laughlin, M. Conreen, H.J. Witchel, and M. Miodownik. 2011. The use of standard electrode potentials to predict the taste of solid metals. *Food Quality and Preference* 22:628-637.

[13] C. Spence and M.K. Ngo. 2012. Assessing the shape symbolism of the taste, flavor, and texture of foods and beverages. *Flavour* 1:12 accessed at http://www.flavourjournal.com.

[14] C. Arnaud. 2011. The synthetic nose. *Chemical and Engineering News* 89(30) 10.

[15] F.H. Chapelle. 2005. *Wellsprings: A Natural History of Bottled Spring Water*. Rutgers University Press, New Brunswick, New Jersey.

[16] C. Spence, L. Richards, E. Kjellin, A. Huhnt, V. Daskal, A. Scheybeler, C. Velasco, and O. Deroy. 2013. Looking for cross modal correspondence between classical music and fine wine. *Flavour* 2:29 accessed at http://www.flavourjournal.com.

Peak Publishing
Golden, Colorado

PEAK PUBLISHING promotes healthier living and whole-some values by publishing resources for the reader's enjoyment, education, or inspiration. We help authors share their stories through memoirs, fiction, biographies, family histories, children's literature, how-to-do-it manuals, educational materials, and more.

Fulfill your dream. Write that book. We can help you reach the world in print and eBook formats.
Contact us at:

1-877-331-2766 | *peakpublishinginfo@gmail.com*

Made in the USA
Middletown, DE
23 December 2017